THE JOHN RYLANDS UNIVERSITY LIBRARY

ARUHT

Living With Grief

Dr Tony Lake

LIVING WITH GRIEF

DR TONY LAKE obtained his Ph.D. in Social Psychology from the University of London in 1972. He is now a private psychotherapist and management communication consultant. He is an accredited counsellor of the British Association for Counselling. His other books include *Loneliness* and *How to Cope with Your Nerves* (both Sheldon Press), and he has written numerous articles for popular magazines as well as academic journals. He has also appeared frequently on both radio and television.

Overcoming Common Problems Series

Overcoming Common Problems

LIVING WITH GRIEF

Dr Tony Lake

SHELDON PRESS
LONDON

85-13727 PT

First published in Great Britain in 1984 by
Sheldon Press, SPCK, Marylebone Road, London NW1 4DU

(ARUHT)

Second impression 1985

Copyright © Dr Tony Lake 1984

All rights reserved. No part of this book may be reproduced or
transmitted in any form or by any means, electronic or
mechanical, including photocopying, recording or by any
information storage or retrieval system, without permission in
writing from the publisher.

JOHN RYLANDS
UNIVERSITY
LIBRARY

157
L 2
b

British Cataloguing in Publication Data

Lake, Tony
    Living with grief.—(Overcoming common problems)
    1. Grief
    I. Title   II. Series
    155.9′37   BF575.G7

    ISBN 0-85969-425-9
    ISBN 0-85969-426-7 Pbk

            Typeset by Inforum Ltd, Portsmouth
            Printed in Great Britain by
        Whitstable Litho Ltd., Whitstable, Kent

BIND

Contents

To my Mother
Gertrude Annie Lake
and to my Father
Bernard Lake

1

The Purposes of Grief

Most of us try to avoid thinking about death, even though we are aware that sooner or later the moment must come when it is time for us to die. In my work as a psychotherapist I have often asked people to picture the kind of death they most want for themselves. They see sunny rooms, full of flowers, a favourite view from the window, and sense the presence of a loved one close by, a person whose being there is important, and who is not expected to do anything except be there. Often they know this person they wish to have near them; sometimes it is a person unknown, a concerned stranger, or somebody as yet unmet. Usually the dying person is in bed, and slips from life into death with no pain. Sometimes people picture themselves dying out of doors, with the cool peace of wind-rippled grass about them, and the sound of the sea close at hand. Whatever scene is described, people nearly always say that they hope their dying will not cause too much distress to those left behind.

Unspoken disquiet

Something unspoken often lies beneath the surface of these conversations. It is not the inevitability of death. Over the years I have come to believe that most of us accept this without the defence of elaborate indifference, and without fear. I know also that most people at the end would like to take over their own dying, and achieve it as an act they have chosen, accepting that their time has come, and having some say in when it shall be. They want a sense of completion to their life. It is from this that the unspoken disquiet seems to arise.

For the fact is that, although we are forced to accept the inevitable finality of our lives, there can be no such inevitability about the manner of our dying. We realise that we may not be able to choose the kind of death we would most like to have. Death can be utterly cruel, wasteful and pointless. It is that fact above all which is hardest to face. For the most part, therefore, we put off thinking about our own death for as long

1

as we can. We know that we will have to face it one day. In a similar way, unless we are forced to do so, we put off thinking about the death of people close to us. Sooner or later, however, with the same inevitability, events force this upon us. We cannot, in life, escape the death of others, just as ultimately we cannot escape our own. And when such moments come to us, we grieve.

The purpose of grief

It is never easy to see a purpose in the death of somebody close to us. Maybe it is pointless to try. There is, however, a purpose in grieving. Its purpose is to enable us, over a period of time, to adapt to what has happened, and to bring us back to life. In the first shock of bereavement we are closer to death than to life. But through our grieving at the loss of those near to us, we can find ways eventually of living closer to life – closer, if our grieving can be complete, than perhaps we have ever lived.

If you have ever asked yourself what is the purpose of life, then maybe you have recognised that most of us do not have a single purpose, but many purposes. Grief renews all the purposes of our lives, whatever these might be. Grief allows us to feel and accept fear, anger, and worry in new ways, and allows us also to experience greater joy and peace. Unlike death itself, grief is never wasteful nor pointless.

Grief for those we love is also an act of completion on their behalf. Through our grief for them, we dedicate a part of our life to completing their life-purposes. At the same time, we draw to a close that part of their life which was shared with us. We find a new perspective from which to see more clearly that part of ourselves which they affected by their life.

A need to learn

The difficulty many of us face is that we know so little about grief until it is upon us. We so often feel inadequate in helping others who are grieving. We face the prospect of having to grieve ourselves with inadequate preparation. Over the last centuries, medical science has found the means to feed and care for people better, to cure illnesses which were once incurable, to push back the frontier of death, so that what was once a commonplace of life is now far rarer. When people lived shorter lives, grieving was better understood. Families were larger, and stayed together more as part of closer communities, so grief was more shared and more public. Men and women who grieved had learned how to grieve as children.

Few of us would regret the passing of those days. We would certainly not wish them back just so we can learn from one another how to grieve, and how to let those around us grieve. We need to find another way. One obviously useful way is to read about grief. I am glad you are doing so. I shall seek to involve you in this book. I hope that we can make this journey together, and that I shall not lose you, nor you lose me.

Being deeply involved

Some of you, I know, are already deeply involved in your own grief. It is not my purpose to comfort you, but rather to be with you as you grow in understanding of your grief, so that as you grow stronger in understanding, so your own greater strength will add to your capacity to take comfort from things around you. When we know what is happening to us, we have more choice in the ways we let it happen.

Suppressed grief

Some of you probably had no intention of reading this book, and are even now wondering whether to go on with it. Maybe the reason you picked it up is that there is a grief buried inside you, and that now at last you feel safe enough to wonder whether you can face it again. Sometimes we cannot deal with our grief at the time its cause occurs. Loss in childhood, bereavement in wartime when close companions are killed, the deaths of ungrown babies – these griefs are amongst those most often thrust down into the secret recesses of our memories to be left intact, waiting for a safe time and place. We are told at the time that these things happen, that life must go on, that we are distressing others by getting things out of proportion. We are advised to forget, and we take the advice by trying hard not to remember. This could have happened to you. If you feel safe enough, you are welcome to join us.

3

Helping others

Maybe you are reading this book as a step towards being better able to help somebody else who is grieving. Like most of us who do such work you probably have your own need to grieve. And you probably also have many questions for which you would like answers. I hope you will find the answers that work best for you either by agreeing with what I say, or disagreeing. From the start it has to be recognised that there is no single set pattern to grief. It serves the purposes of the personalities it affects. So there is little value in authoritative statements about how somebody should grieve, whether their grief is 'normal' or 'abnormal', how long grief lasts 'on average', or what should be said to help somebody 'get over it'. The way to understand a grief is to understand the person who has it, and the relationship he or she had with the grieved-for person. The best way to help is to be a better listener – and plenty will be said about that.

Knowledge and wisdom

It is not always a person who is grieved for. Grief, in its widest sense, is the reaction to significant loss. We shall concentrate mainly on the grief which comes from the death of people close to us, but it is also important to recognise that grief can be just as great when a much loved pet dies, when an accident or serious surgery deprives a person of part of his or her body, when some relationships break up, as in divorce, when people are separated for the last time from places they love, or objects they deeply value. It is common for the mistake to be made that grief is only real when it arises from the death of a person.

From time immemorial each generation has had a need to learn afresh about grief. Today, we can use the study of human behaviour to help us understand the way we live our lives and how much we need one another. The second way of learning about grief is the old way, directly through our experiences and our feelings. This is the way of knowing grief, rather than knowing *about* it. The first way leads us to knowledge, the second way to wisdom. We need both; to think and to feel. And we need to face the old questions, the questions of life and death.

4

Inner commitment

We live, you and I, in an ordered, relatively well-regulated way. Because of this we can take things for granted. We expect to own our own clothes, to have a roof over our heads, a bed to sleep in each night. We might have to think about what we will eat tonight, or next week, and plan the cooking and the shopping. We may worry from time to time about where the money will come from to buy the things we need. But we tend to take for granted that we will not starve, or be left totally penniless, although this happens to some people. The overwhelming majority of those of us who live in the safe, wealthy nations of the earth are used to making plans, having choices, and living our lives within the broad expectation of being reasonably happy. We are able generally to avoid thinking about death until we come into contact with it. We also tend to avoid thinking about life, too. When we gather together in families, or as groups of friends, our conversation scarcely touches our deepest concerns, unless we are troubled. To talk about life and death issues would be seen as too heavy or too presumptuous. Deep matters make people feel uncomfortable.

Yet it seems to me that although we do not spend much of our time in general thinking about life and what it means, each one of us, in our own way, shows a certain degree of commitment to life itself. Some people seem to be one hundred per cent committed to life. Others seem fifty per cent committed to it. Yet others seem hardly committed at all. In between the two extremes of all or nothing at all, lie many variations. The degree of commitment shows in the liveliness of the person – some are full of living, some are less so. It seems to make no difference whether the person is rich or poor, healthy or ill, lucky or unlucky. Some people seem full of life even in the worst adversity.

Life or death

But those people who are less than fully committed to life seem to me to have partially given in to death. They have accepted discouragement, and decided that for a certain part of their time, life is not worth living. Maybe they feel this way at work, and come to life again when they get home. Perhaps they spend most of their time just getting through from one hour to the next, unable to recall the last time they experienced boundless joy or felt their spirits touched by the magic of something beautiful. How does this come about? Sometimes people are discouraged in childhood, brought up by parents who themselves had little or no reason to expect life to be worth living except for the occasional short-lived pleasure. When such people grow up, they expect from life only what their parents expected, and never question the rightness of their discouragement.

Perhaps others of us, as we go through life, are deeply affected by events which frighten us or anger us, so that in the crisis that arises we are forced to think about ourselves and our lives. Then we question our commitment, and resolve from the inner knowledge of how much courage we have, whether we want to live or die. We can stay permanently discouraged, or renew our commitment to life.

Whatever the cause of a human crisis, there is often a low point in the life of the sufferer when he or she has to decide whether to live or die. Maybe (if there is such a person) he or she who has never known deep suffering will not understand this. But those who have been deeply hurt and come through will recognise the feeling of having chosen life and rejected death. It is a choice we can only make for ourselves, within ourselves. People often experience a deep sense of tranquillity once they have decided, whatever they decide. It is as though they have stopped trying to do the impossible, and can now rest.

Somebody with you

When you are faced with such a decision, only you can make it. Nobody else can do it for you. In that sense you are alone. Yet it often helps to have somebody with you at the time – somebody who will simply be there, who will not try to influence your decision, or do anything about what you decide. It is just that the presence of another person can sometimes help us when we are most deeply afraid. It is one of the tragedies of life that such people are not always there, and one of the glories of life that they sometimes are.

Reward

The old question of life or death, therefore, lies at the core of our deepest crises. Those who face such crises and choose life, and are able to build surely upon that foundation, emerge as stronger people, more full of life than before. The more doubts they can resolve, the stronger they become. People who have never doubted, and who have never faced the old question and resolved it seem, by comparison, to be less substantial, in some way less complete. They appear to spend their lives on the surface of events, paddling rather than swimming, knowledgeable and useful, but as yet untouched by the mature wisdom that comes from deep commitment. That more solid value which men and women bring with them out of crisis is a part of the wisdom which throughout the ages has been respected and loved amongst their fellow humans. Much of it comes from the experience of knowing grief. It is the reward of a completed grieving.

2

The Tasks of Grieving

The idea that every one of us can become more fulfilled through our experience of grief may seem strange to you, particularly if you have never thought about it before. Grief is generally thought of as being a feeling of unmitigated unhappiness. So, at first sight, it seems contradictory to suggest that it can lead to people having a deeper capacity for real happiness. Why do we tend to reject the idea, and why, instead of rejecting it, should we accept it?

Maybe most of us who reject the notion do so from feelings of guilt. We feel revulsion at the thought of obtaining fulfilment for ourselves through something as tragic as the loss of somebody we love. Profiting in any way from such an event seems too close to the idea that we wanted it to happen.

Nevertheless, the proposition that grief can be a strengthening experience makes a great deal of sense. Ask yourself about your own death. Would you want the people you leave behind to be perpetually miserable, and you to have caused that misery by your death? If we are honest about it, most of us will admit to wanting people to be sad that we have died, but we also want them to be glad they knew us, and to be able to be happier in some way as a result of our life. We would not want them to be for ever miserable because of us when we are dead.

And we also need to ask whether it is really possible for the death of somebody near to us to be the sole cause of our being for ever unhappy. If we spend the rest of our life being miserable, surely a large part of the responsibility for this reaction must be our own. How can we blame it on the death of that person? To say that another person's death has caused this is ultimately no different from blaming that person for causing our unhappiness by dying. We cause a very large part of our own unhappiness, but we are not always honest enough with ourselves to be able to face up to this responsibility.

There are sometimes, of course, people in our lives who seem to spend a great deal of their time making us feel anxious or angry, who can belittle us and trap us into feeling impotent rage or are the apparent cause of interminable worry. In life they seem to want us to be unhappy. But when such a person dies, and we grieve for them, we have a new chance to decide whether or not we want to go on being unhappy because it was what he or she wanted of us.

Although a sense of guilt may make us want to reject the idea at first, the death of somebody close to us always brings new choices into our life. It is up to us to make the kinds of choices that help us, and those who depend upon us. Usually the person who has died would have wanted this as well. But if not, then his or her death will have set us free to do so in any case.

The pathway of grief

The generally accepted view that grief means being desperately unhappy needs to be challenged in another way, too. Grief is not a simple matter of being unhappy. Grieving people feel the normal range of feelings that anyone else has. They are not turned overnight into strange beings who cannot laugh at a joke, enjoy food, sleep soundly, make love, argue about politics, thoroughly enjoy an evening out. Indeed, if we treat those who are grieving as if they were incapable of fun, then we merely hurt them more, by rejecting them when they most need us to be by their side simply being ourselves.

The most important point to recognise is that grief is not just something that happens to you, when a person near you dies. It is not just a patch of misery which you encounter and have to get through as quickly as possible with the help of friends who take your mind off it. It is something you *do*, not something which happens to you – an active process, or pathway for you to follow, a journey for which you are responsible, and not a passive event caused by circumstances beyond your control. *You* are the only person who can identify and then carry out the purposes of your own grieving.

Living with grief means that you, as a grieving person, have certain tasks to face as part of your own life. Each one will take time, and space, and energy. There will be occasions when you despair, because these resources do not seem available to you. And there will be times when you are aware of having accomplished significant changes in your life. You can only successfully carry out each of the tasks of your own grief

9

when you are ready to do so. In the meantime, you are essentially the same person you have been from the start.

It is the accomplishment of the tasks of grieving that leads from bereavement and the deep shock and sadness of loss, to the eventual achievement of greater fulfilment. Leaving these tasks undone merely saves them for later. Surely, if they have to be done, then it is best to tackle them with courage.

Different kinds of task

But what are they? Obviously, the tasks of grief will differ in detail from one individual to the next. But, in principle, they are the same for everybody the world over. We can therefore make very useful generalisations about them, so that by applying the principles that underlie them to your own circumstances, you can gain new insight into your own very particular needs.

There are two sets of tasks that we need to look at in this way. First there are the tasks to do with *acceptance*. Realising what to accept, and how to accept them, is the key to completing such tasks. Secondly, there is a group of tasks which I have called the 'tasks of *resistance*'. These are about the things grieving people need to fight against. We shall also need to consider the special circumstances which surround the grieving person. For example, there are many very useful general things we can say at this stage which arise because the person who is grieved for died in a particular way, or had a particular kind of relationship with the grieving person.

In considering the tasks of grief, we need to recognise that the problems which face the grieving person frequently have a long history. Those things we need to accept about ourselves, and the things we need to fight against, are often rooted deep in our past, in the childhood influences that helped to shape our lives, or in the decisions of adolescence and early adult life that led us towards the relationship we built over the years with the person we have now lost. Bereavement frequently means that issues we may have avoided for a very long time rise to the surface again. If we face up to the tasks of grief, then we will accept this and try to do something about those issues.

10

The problems of acceptance

The contrast between life as it is and life as we would most like it to be affects each one of us to some extent – whether we are grieving or not. When we are completely happy, there seems to be no gap between the two. At other times there may be a slight gap, no more than a minor irritant or occasional sense of frustration. But our lives can also go through passages when nothing that we want seems to be available to us.

To make changes in your life – to be successful in turning what you have into what you would like to have, is always difficult. Inside most of us there is a strong fear of change. We know that to alter our circumstances in any radical way means altering ourselves first, doing the things we have always been scared to do in spite of that terror we will feel, taking risks we dare not take. It means becoming somebody different from the person we have always been up to now.

Should we accept the way things are, or should we try to change them? That is the quandary which lies behind all such problems. To accept things which we dislike about ourselves or our circumstances might condemn us to a way of life which we can barely tolerate, but which we will never change. It might mean spending the rest of our life in regret. At the same time, if we try to change things and fail, we might make matters worse. We can only break this deadlock if we can somehow attain a clear-sighted understanding of what can be changed, and what can not. Only then can we 'realise' change, that is concentrate our energy in a realistic way upon those things which are worth trying to achieve, and accept that we will have to live with those unpleasant facts of life that we cannot change.

The full reality

When you are grieving, whatever the reasons for your grief, you are faced with the need to adapt to what has happened, and to do this realistically. You were close to somebody, and that person is now dead. At first it can be very hard to accept that this is so. The straightforward biological fact is the least complicated aspect of the new reality you face. To accept the full reality, with all its implications, is far harder. At first you

11

do not know all the implications. And they do not emerge tidily or neatly arranged in order of importance. Assessing the full nature of the impact which your bereavement has upon you is an immense task – lengthy, complicated and exhausting. When you go through the process of sorting out what has happened to you, the contrast between the way things are and the way you would like them to be can be overwhelming – because you have to decide what aspects of your new circumstances can be altered, and whether you want to alter them.

If it were just a matter of accepting the death of somebody, and learning how to readjust to all the consequences of that event, then the task would be daunting. But there is even more to it than that. The people for whom we grieve are usually the ones who have been an important part of our life for a long time. There may have been changes we could have made which were not made because of them. So we may need to go through a complete reappraisal not just of the present and the future it will lead to, but also of the past and what it has done to us as a direct result of our relationship with the person who has died.

The need to go on

Accepting the reality of loss, with all its consequences for what we do and what we are, is not the only acceptance task that faces us when we grieve. The future can seem empty. We feel at such times that there is nothing for us in that direction. We are struggling in vain, and the realistic, objective fact is that we are wasting our time and everybody else's in even trying to go on. If we give in, and find a way effectively of ending our connection with life, so be it. The struggle would be over. It is this need to decide whether or not to go on which forms the second task of acceptance – the task of accepting the need to go on. If we fail at this task, when the crisis comes, our grief will have defeated us. Death – by this mechanism – is contagious.

Help

We also need to accept that we need help. For some of us this is the hardest task of all. Many of us have been trained from childhood to hide the distress we feel inside. Men are often brought up to believe that there is something unforgivable about crying, something so bad that once they give way to their sorrow and weep openly, they will lose for ever after their right to be called men. Many women have been taught to cope – that is, to find enough courage from somewhere to be able to pretend that they do not need help, and so successfully avoid being a 'burden'.

Of course, there are wide variations in all this. Many men can cry, and many women are able to see that coping is not enough. But we are all of us brought up from childhood to set limits on how much help we are willing to accept. One of the tasks of grief we are forced to face is the necessity of deciding whether the limits we have always been used to setting ourselves still apply. Maybe they do. Maybe we have never asked for help and we would be wrong to do so now. Maybe the help available would cost us too dear, or would be inadequate. But we have to decide, or grief will be harder to bear.

A struggle

Accepting the reality of the loss with all its implications in terms of the past, present, and future, accepting the need to go on, and accepting the need for help – these are the main tasks of *acceptance* which face us when we grieve. Not one of these tasks is simple and straightforward. In each case it means we have to take complicated decisions about whether we are being realistic or not. Acceptance is a constant struggle to connect with reality, and to stay in contact with it, so that our actions can steadily increase the extent of our freedom from illusion. It is the casting aside of the fantasies which up to now have protected us from change. Often it is no more than a fragile act of faith that although something we seem to have striven for all our lives can now no longer be obtained, we are still here, and still alive, and still have a future illuminated by the candle-flicker of a little hope.

The problems of resistance

So far, we have looked at the tasks which arise in principle because of the gap which often exists between life as it is and

13

life as we would most like it to be. There is often a similar contrast in our lives between the way people perceive us, and the way we know ourselves to be. At the simplest level, for example, there are many adults whose parents still treat them as young children, not as fully mature men and women in their own right. There are women who are perceived solely as 'Mum', not just by their children, but also by their husbands. And there are men, women and children whose work brings them into contact daily with very powerful people who have fixed ideas about their capability which directly contradict the inner knowledge which those people have of themselves.

Problems of *resistance* arise whenever we insist on going against the fixed ideas and expectations people have about us. The grown-up son or daughter refuses to play the game of being little boy or girl. The duty visits, the weekly phone call full of platitudes to keep the parents quiet, the passive acceptance of the parents' right to question any major decision, however well thought-out – these features of the relationship are challenged. The parent is told that they are no longer acceptable, or if he or she is not told, this fact is made clear in other ways.

Similarly, the woman who insists on being treated as a person in her own right is resisting expectations others have of her – perhaps those of her children or her husband, or maybe expectations other women or men might have of her. People at work or school who stop behaving the way they are expected to behave, or who resist meeting the expectations of their managerial superiors are also involved in similar conflicts. Resistance to the fixed ideas others have of us always produces conflict.

Dramatic change

Like the problems of acceptance, those which arise from our need to resist other people's expectations from time to time, are general 'life problems', and not ones which apply exclusively to grieving people. But when a person close to you dies, the degree to which you are affected by such problems can change dramatically. A couple of examples will help to illustrate this point. Somebody who was always seen as wife and mother, and whose opportunities to be treated as a person in

14

her own right were limited by this, might feel quite contented with such an arrangement. Maybe she accepts it because she likes it, because it helps her feel safe and wanted, because it is all she has known for many years. But when her husband dies, she has to change from carrying out the role of wife to the far less certain role of widow. She is still 'Mother', but no longer as part of a living partnership with her husband. Suddenly she may find that her children treat her more as a burden than as an asset. She may need to carve out a new niche for herself, to resist the expectations her children have of her. And this will not be possible without conflict.

Suppose, as another example, that the youngest daughter of several children in a grown up family looks after the widowed father. The family as a whole is mildly supportive, but gains more from the arrangement than it contributes. The woman's brothers and sisters have for years left their father's affairs in her hands. Hardly anybody has thought of her as a person in her own right. Then the old man dies. Suddenly her position will have changed from that of being the person who saved the family from a problem, to being a major potential problem to her brothers and sisters. How is she to react?

Resisting pressure

These are just two examples of the way people can go on for many years never challenging the assumptions other people make about them, and then find that they are faced with a choice because of bereavement. On the one hand they can do what everybody else expects of them, whatever that is. On the other, they can resist pressure from other people to conform to expectations. The first way may mean continuing to give up your chances of being a person in your own right, even though the main reasons for doing so disappeared when your bereavement happened. The second way, however, means facing the anger and anxiety of the people whose expectations you will have to disappoint. And you will have to do this at a time when you already feel vulnerable because of the bereavement. People who grieve have been forced by events to look rather more deeply at their lives, and to re-examine their life-purposes and their relationships. Whether we like it or not, this is an angry world. There are many people who expect you to be what they want you to be because it suits them. They choose roles for you – casting you in their own life-dramas, so you can play a supporting part to their star performances. And it goes deeper than this. Our relationships from childhood help to shape us in the image which suits those who have power over us. If we resist these expectations others have of us, then there are sanctions, some gentle, some severe and ruthless, designed to bring us back into line. Maybe you will disagree with me, or think me inordinately cynical, but my own experience is that people are often persuaded to give up their money or to sacrifice love, but they are seldom willing to give up power unless they are forced to do so by evidence of superior power.

Conflict and isolation

The tasks of resistance which face the grieving person call into question the power of other people over that person. That is why they always run the risk of producing conflict. The power of the family will inevitably be used to try to force the grieving person into line if he or she fails to meet their expectations. The widow whose children want to see her as for ever in mourning for Dad will shock and anger those children if she starts to look around for a new mate. They will try to force her to be what they want her to be. The widower who suddenly produces a girl-friend at a gathering of his married children will probably stimulate an angry, partly hidden debate about her suitability.

When you are grieving, the people around you have their own needs to stop you behaving as a person in your own right. It is essential for you to face up to the question of whether or not to resist the pressure they will use to make you do things their way. Much of it may seem very kindly, full of sincere concern for you. But you still have to ask yourself whether what they want for you is really what you want for yourself.

The greatest dangers come from failure to resist the isolation which grief so often brings, because other people may be shocked if you are seen to be enjoying yourself, or building a new life for yourself. Part of grieving means recognising your new need to be independent, and resisting other people's interference and opposition. You need to resist the tyranny of the living. And, by slowly freeing yourself from the past, and building a new future for yourself, you need also to resist the tyranny of the past.

3

A Special Relationship

When we face the tasks of grief we do so with an added element of difficulty which reflects the unique circumstances of our own relationship with the person we have lost. At one extreme, for example, a relationship can be such that the person left behind seems unable to grieve at all. In other cases, the grief of the survivor may seem insurmountable. It is generally assumed in everyday life that if somebody you would expect to grieve feels quite unable to do so, there was probably something unhappy about their relationship. Also, if a person seems to be inconsolable as a result of a bereavement, it is popularly supposed that there must have been great love between them. Most of us, from our own experience of people, are aware that grief is difficult for some people to start at all, hard for some to get over, and – in very rare cases – accepted and lived through by the survivors with a sense of great peace and joy. How can we account for these differences? What is it about a relationship that could result in the bereaved person having extreme difficulty either starting or finishing grief? What kind of relationship would result in almost joyful grief?

There can be no complete answer to these questions. As far as I know, neither medical nor psychological research has produced any scientific evidence to account for the differences. My own opinion, based on my experience as a counsellor, and shared by many of the counsellors I have spoken to, is that one very important factor is the extent to which the feelings people have for one another are hidden from one another. Deep feelings are often suppressed in our everyday relationships. They may be feelings of antagonism – irritation, frustration, anger, contempt – or they may be feelings of deep love and affection. For example, I have often met married couples, who, for various reasons, dislike one another deeply enough for a divorce to seem very likely, yet who go on living together and denying the antagonistic feelings they have towards one another. I have met many men and women who will admit privately to disliking intensely members of their own family but who skilfully conceal this from them for a

18

variety of reasons. And I vividly recall a thirty-year-old man who adored his grandfather, but who had never been able to tell him for fear of embarrassing him.

Love and power

Relationships in which both people can unreservedly accept one another, in which they do not try to change one another in any way, and where they are able to give to and receive from one another complete and unconditional love, are very rare. Indeed they are so rare that most of us would consider them to be ideal, but probably unattainable on any lasting basis. In such a relationship the partners do not seek to control one another. By contrast, the relationships which most of us have are based on mixed feelings which we do not examine very deeply. Although we may love somebody, there may be times when we dislike their behaviour. We are not 'perfect', and neither are those we love. So we do not, on the whole, expect our relationships to be perfect. Our antagonisms surface from time to time but, after they have had a brief airing, we bottle them up again.

And there are many of our marital, and family relationships in which what passes for love is really power. Love means giving without counting the cost. Power means treating the other person as an investment or as an object – a good or poor investment, a precious or rather inferior object. Love would mean complete acceptance, yet few of us give this, and few of us receive it. We tend to invest our energy trying to change people – children particularly. When all our hard work fails to produce the desired result, we lose patience and apply force. We tend to forget that they are people in their own right, thus denying to them the essential dignity of being fully responsible for their own lives.

I am not saying that perfect love is impossible for all of us – I do not know. But I am convinced that beneath the surface of many of our normal, acceptable, loving relationships, there are many hidden destructive feelings. We get by from day to day in spite of this, by not admitting these feelings to one another, and often by not admitting them to ourselves.

19

Disturbing effect

It is for the people with whom we share these everyday mixed relationships that we are most likely to grieve. They are our husbands and wives, our lovers, our brothers and sisters, our parents, our children and our close friends and neighbours. When we are faced with accepting the full reality of our loss, the full reality is that we have lost a mixture. We have lost the good things that we received from the relationship. We have also lost bad things which may have forced us to keep anger or fear hidden away inside us. Now that the reason for hiding these feelings is no longer there in the same degree, they are harder to keep bottled up. We begin to feel disturbed by them in a new way. We find ourselves having to reassess all our feelings. Were the good feelings we had worth the price we paid? The gap between life as we wanted it to be, life as we pretended it to be, and life as it really is, can be very disturbing when we begin to examine it closely.

Dependence

In this way, hidden feelings in a relationship which has now been irrevocably altered by bereavement, can add to the difficulty of accepting the full reality of loss. Such feelings can also make it harder for the grieving person to accept the need to go on. A mixture of power and love usually means that the people in such a relationship are very dependent upon one another – they have invested a great deal in their relationship. So mixed in with the sadness, the feelings of shared pain and distress, there is often also a terrible fear of the future that the surviving partner must now face alone. He or she may be quite unused to independence. 'What shall I do without him?' 'How can I survive without her?' These questions are a frequent cry from the heart of the bereaved. They show how hard it is in many cases to accept the need to go on living when it all seems so hopeless and lonely and pointless.

Betrayal and embarrassment

Even the need to accept help is made harder by the mixed feelings of many ordinary, intimate, very special relationships.

To admit to oneself the bad feelings that may have been bottled up for years is hard enough. But to admit them to strangers or to relatives from whom the truth has also been hidden, can seem almost impossible. It would be a betrayal, an embarrassment. It might also shock the helper. Helpers are often people who do not want to hear the truth, or who feel obliged to make moral judgements about what they hear, and then offer advice. So there are grieving people whose hidden feelings prevent them from asking for the help they need.

Retreat into loneliness

Hidden feelings can also increase the difficulty grieving people have in resisting isolation. Isolation can take many forms. There is the physical isolation of ill-health, for example. It is not uncommon for grieving people to allow ill-health to take over – to stop resisting it. This is often related to an awareness that there is nobody around now who understands the way they are – who can take account of their need to have their mixture of feelings understood, even when they do not themselves understand the mixture. The person who has died would have understood, or at least, reacted in a way which the grieving person could predict and respond to without effort. But now there are only people around who have to have explanations. It is easier to try not to resist, to have a headache, to suffer from the old back pain, to stay in bed feeling ill, to feel 'not quite up to things'. Illness becomes a mixture of reality and excuse – real pain given in to, as an excuse to isolate yourself from people to whom you cannot explain your hidden feelings.

Another kind of physical isolation that can be made worse by hidden feelings is sexual isolation. People who have lost husbands, wives, or lovers whose touch they have grown used to over many years need to understand their own need for intimate touch, and find new ways of meeting this need. Yet their own hidden feelings – for example that nobody else could possibly find them attractive – may prevent them from resisting isolation.

Loneliness in the bereaved often seems to me to stem from a deep-seated reluctance on their part to accept that other people can understand the way they are – the way they feel,

21

the value of their life experience, their idiosyncrasies – now that their partners are not around any more. We need people to talk to whom we can see as our kind of people. But if we are not sure what this is, then it can be easier to stop looking than to resist the intellectual and social isolation we feel. So a bit of us dies. Part of us, we feel, will never be the same again, never be valued again. We reduce our commitment to life, and death wins another small victory.

Delaying grief

So far we have looked at the effects of suppressed feelings on people who are, nevertheless, able to begin their grieving soon after the bereavement. Not being sure how they felt deep inside towards the person who has died makes grief harder for them to get through. They grieve for longer than they would otherwise have done, and they are more prone to setbacks. But in a sense they are luckier than those who feel quite unable to grieve. It will be helpful at this stage to look at an example of this – where grief was delayed for forty years. Throughout the whole of this time the person could not start his grieving, and a part of him was therefore unable to live fully.

Forty years

A few months before this book was written, I was helping to train a group of people in counselling skills – the skills of being a good listener so that people who want to reassess what is happening in their lives have someone they can talk to who will not make judgements but simply help them think aloud and decide what to do. The man I shall call Ron was a member of that group. He was there because the company he worked for had asked him to help people who were approaching retirement. He was about sixty years old, a tall, gentle, attractive man, with that rare ability to let people be themselves which is the hallmark of a naturally excellent listener. As part of the training course the participants were teamed up in pairs to gain experience both as counsellor and client – to practise being better listeners, and also to have an opportunity themselves to reassess some aspect of their life which was impor-

22

tant to them. Ron chose to talk about an incident which had taken place forty years before.

He began by saying that he felt troubled by something that had happened to him when he was not quite twenty-one years old. It had bothered him intermittently ever since, and lately he had found his mind dwelling on it more and more. He wanted to talk about it so that he would feel better. It was not, he hastened to add, something he felt very strongly about. He would not like it to be thought that he had a big problem.

I was sitting in the next room while he said this, along with several of his colleagues who were on the course. We were watching by means of a closed circuit television link which Ron was fully aware of but which he now seemed to be ignoring completely as he became absorbed in his feelings. As Ron denied the importance of the problem, we exchanged glances, acknowledging amongst ourselves the presence in Ron of powerful, hidden emotions.

One mistake

Ron talked about his life at that time. He was a bomber pilot, flying Lancasters from an airfield in eastern England on night-time raids into Germany. The loss of life from these raids was such that his chances of survival were, in actuarial terms at least, non-existent. Ron was an insurance man and knew the risk he ran. In matter-of-fact terms he told how he had tried to give his crew the best chance. He ruled with a rod of iron, doing everything by the book, judging whether or not a crew member was good enough with no sentiment. Anybody who did not come up to his standards was out. It only took one mistake, and Ron would ruthlessly ensure that the person concerned never flew with them again. 'Maybe I was too harsh', he said, 'but I had to be cruel. People hated me at times, but I survived.' 'Did you have *any* friends?', asked his counsellor. 'My friend died,' answered Ron.

There had been a crew-member, his navigator. He was a couple of years older than Ron, and had 'shown him the ropes' when he first joined the squadron. Ron remembered him as full of life, always cheerful. One night the bomber returned in flames, with Ron nursing it along and only his navigator and he still alive. They almost made it to the airfield. Ron was thrown clear, and found himself in a ditch, standing up to his waist in water some fifty yards away while the aircraft burned. 'If only I'd been quicker,' he said. 'I just seemed to stand there. I could have got him out. I keep thinking, I could have got him out.'

Failure

As we watched, we could see that his face was angry. He went on to explore this feeling. He was furious with himself, to have let everybody down in this way. At the time people had told him not to blame himself. They hadn't understood – his had been an unpardonable error, a bad piece of flying, a lapse of self-discipline in not getting a hold of himself after the crash. Yet he had not been punished. 'Maybe you have punished yourself?' asked the counsellor. 'But what I can't understand is why,' said Ron. 'Why did I let it happen? Why can't I accept what they said?' The two sat for a while in silence. Then Ron said that he had never wept about the incident. He had felt only anger at his failure.

Later, when the practice session was over, and Ron joined his colleagues, he was asked to say more about his friend. 'How did you feel about him?' Somebody put the question a different way – 'Did you love him?' Ron sat very still. 'I suppose I did,' he replied. 'Yes – I did.' And he began to weep, for the first time in forty years, because he felt safe enough to grieve over his friend.

Ron had not been free to grieve before because he had been unable to acknowledge to himself or his closest friend the feelings of deep affection and admiration he had felt. There had been no room in his life at that time for anything as weakening and dangerous as caring about a fellow human being. His strategy for survival would have been fatally undermined. He had not dared to deflect himself from his main purpose – to be a ruthless, efficient machine, a man without feelings. Yet he had failed. He was human after all, but could not admit this to himself. The failure that hurt him most had not been his inability to save the aircraft, or the man inside it. It had been his failure to prevent himself caring about what happened to one of his crew. Now he could begin to live with this failure, to accept it at last, because he had realised

24

that he needed to hide this feeling no longer.

Something else

If you had feelings about the person you have lost which could
not be dealt with as part of your living relationship with him or
her, then these have to be dealt with as part of your grief. The
more such feelings have been hidden, the harder it will be to
find them and to assess what they mean to you, unless you
have help.

Grieving is harder for each individual to the extent that
there are hidden feelings. There is also something else which
can add to the difficulty, and that is the particular circumstances of how the death happened. We need to face up to the
fact at this point that when a person dies, his or her way of
dying can cause you hardship in itself. It can leave you singu-
larly unprepared for grieving, or alter the way you think about
him or her. Later we shall look at this in greater detail, but
before we do so, it will help us to see why it is in general that
the way some deaths happen can make our grieving very much
harder.

A long fatal illness

When somebody dies after a long illness, the time which leads
up to this death is often very difficult for those who care about
the person. They have to find reserves of energy far beyond
the normal demands made on them, and they would not be
human if they did not find themselves resenting this sometimes. For many people the strain of not knowing what is
happening, always being unsure about how long it will last,
and staying as cheerful as possible would be hard enough to
bear; but there may also be a long succession of tiring jour-
neys to a hospital, and worry about the impact the time
required is having on their job or their finances. Sometimes
the dying person is a help through all this strain. Sometimes he
or she, and those who will grieve, draw closer together.

But this may not happen. The dying person may not want
this, due to inner feelings of fear or anger. Or the nature of the
illness may prevent it from happening. Towards the end,

elderly people may regress into a kind of childlike state, a senile dementia which means they do not recognise those who have come to show they care. They may say hurtful things to you, in the mistaken impression that they are talking to somebody else about you. They may cause you and the nursing staff a great deal of worry by wandering around and doing mischievous deeds. They can make you feel ashamed of them, angry with them, distant from them – and you are quite likely to cope with this only by pretending that it is not really happening to you.

When you lose somebody as a result of a long, wasting illness, such as cancer, it is often very hard to keep the reality alive in your mind of what this person was once like. The disease changes the way he or she looks, and behaves. Medication never quite dulls the pain continuously and you inevitably feel for somebody who is close to you and who is in pain. You can find yourself living from day to day, neglecting the future. Death in the end may seem a relief, and this feeling can conflict with the sadness that you always expected to feel. Only if you can use this time of their dying to form a better relationship with your loved ones can you face the tasks of grieving more easily.

Accident and sudden death

Grieving for somebody who has died a sudden, unexpected death can be especially difficult, both when that death was the result of an unsuspected or sudden illness, and when it was the result of a violent accident or the violent intentional action of another person. Things are left unsaid. There can be no saying of goodbyes. Quarrels which might have been resolved only hours later are interrupted, and might be for ever left unresolved.

Grief means that, on behalf of the dead person, we complete their life in some way. This is easier when that life ended in a way that we ourselves might have chosen – not necessarily free from pain, but certainly not upon the rack of cruel and unwonted emotional torment. Violent and unexpected dying can make us feel not just lonely and incomplete when we think of the person we have lost, but also awaken a horror in us that he or she went through so much torment and perhaps we were not there. We may then feel a sense of having been rejected from the event, of having been cheated and excluded. The violence of a death can be reflected in a violent grieving, full of angry self-rejection and guilt.

Children

The death of children is also especially hard to bear. Perhaps the love we feel towards children, particularly when they are very young, is something they do not themselves fully understand, and which is therefore not easy to acknowledge openly on both sides. We do not always tell our children that we love them, and this may be because they would not understand all that we would mean. And perhaps we do not fully understand it ourselves. Love for a child can be a mixture of many feelings. The loss of a child can bring to the surface fears that you have failed in your caring, as well as grief at the loss of somebody with a life of his or her own that you have shared in.

Grieving for the ungrown also involves us in an act of completion in repect of a life which never contained the experiences of maturity. There are birthdays and Christmases he or she will never see, and each of these occasions will be a sad anniversary. But neither will he or she have babies, enjoy the accomplishments of middle life, or be by your side when you are old. You may feel you have more to do in your act of completion on behalf of somebody ungrown than for somebody who has lived a full life.

The tasks of acceptance are hardest when you feel that life has been unfair. And the tasks of resistance following the loss particularly of a baby before or just after birth are complicated by another factor which we need to acknowledge here. Over generations of commonplace infantile and perinatal mortality, people have put pressure on grieving mothers and fathers to get over it quickly. Grieving mothers are, even these days, rushed into another pregnancy, to 'help them forget'. Fathers who do not 'decently' suppress their grief are often thought of as 'odd'. Pressure from family and friends, even from doctors, can lead to either or both parents hiding their real feelings and becoming isolated from one another, yet unable to seek help. They may sincerely believe they are helping one another, but they are actually delaying the shared, healing grief which would bring them closer together.

Not at peace

There are other circumstances which bring added difficulty which we shall discuss in detail later – the special problems of the death of a parent, for example. But there is another particular difficulty we need to mention here, and that is the grief we accord to those who take their own life. From time to time you or I may have felt our way through the kind of crisis which others resolve by suicide. We might be able to understand that despair or anger which leads to somebody ending his own life by killing himself. If so, then it will be easier to see that death by one's own hand is a statement about one's life.

For those who grieve when somebody close to them has committed suicide, there is the added difficulty of having to interpret this statement. We struggle to comprehend why they chose this way, what they were saying to us, whether we were responsible and in what way. It may have been anger with us that led them to it, or anger with other people as well, perhaps with life itself. Or it may have been fear of something they could have faced with our help if we had been nearer to their inner feelings. And all that has been said earlier about sudden violent death applies here also. Children who die in this way bring that extra burden too. When we grieve after a suicide our need to feel at peace becomes terrifyingly acute because we know that the person we grieve for was not at peace with us. Even if we have known this for a long time, our need is still much harder to meet.

4

Realisation

When the human body is faced with any rapid and potentially overwhelming demand upon its resources, it protects itself by going into shock. Each individual is affected differently – some show more physical symptoms than others. For anything from a few moments to several days, the individual cannot really grasp what has happened.

Shock is usually our first reaction to finding out that somebody very important to us has died. Even if we have known for a long time that he or she was going to die, even if we are present when it happens, we will probably go into shock for a few moments. Being given the news unexpectedly by somebody else is likely to produce a stronger reaction so that the first realisation is delayed even longer. There are, of course, horrific circumstances under which shock is extreme, usually because there are other reasons for it, such as a road accident in which someone you love dies, and in which you may also suffer severe physical injuries. The degree of shock experienced can be thought of as depending upon the extent of the demand which the event makes upon the person's resources. This determines how far it is necessary for the person's automatic defences to protect him.

Perhaps the most important task which we all have to face when we grieve, is to accept the reality of our loss. It is this process that shock protects us from at first. But as we recover from the automatic protection our bodies impose upon us, we begin to try consciously to 'realise' what has happened. What is involved in this process of 'realisation', and how can we use an understanding of the process to help ourselves?

The pattern of realisation

I believe that if we look carefully at the reaction of people as they come out of shock and they begin to understand, we can see a pattern in what happens. This pattern is repeated over and over again during the ensuing weeks and months. It seems to me worthwhile to understand the pattern, so we can have a clearer idea of what happens to us. We shall also be better

29

equipped to understand, and therefore to help, other people.

To illustrate what I mean by the 'pattern', I shall refer to a real person – let us call her Joyce – to whom I acted as counsellor during the early stages of grief after her husband died. We shall use her story to look in detail first at the process of realising that somebody has died.

Joyce's husband died of a heart attack shortly after being taken ill at the house of a friend of the family. It was this friend who telephoned her with the news. Her friend said on the telephone that she was going to drive the eighty or so miles from the hospital immediately to be with Joyce. She also said she was going to phone Joyce's next-door neighbour and tell her the news, and that she would ask this person to come round and wait with Joyce. The friend, whom I shall call Helen, arrived about an hour and a half later.

At this stage, if we are to understand what Joyce felt, we need to ask ourselves some questions. Why was Joyce's husband at Helen's house? When had he had the attack? Was it likely that a heart attack could have resulted in him dying so soon? There is an almost endless list of things we do not know which help us make sense of what had happened.

A Small part of reality

Joyce was faced in real life with just as many questions. She could not take them all in. She knew her husband was away on a business trip, but she had not expected him to call and see Helen. Helen was the same age as both she and her husband – a former secretary of his from a previous job as sales director of a company. He had given Joyce no reason to suspect that he might be prone to heart illness. But although Joyce in real life obviously knew far more about her circumstances than we can, everything she knew seemed totally uncertain because of what had happened. Her list of possible questions was endless too.

How could her mind cope with all the possibilities? It did so the way any other mind does – it fastened upon a small part of the reality. As Helen arrived, and Joyce began to emerge from shock, all Joyce could try to take in was the fact that Helen said that something terrible had happened to Joyce's husband. She might have doubted the truth of this until she saw

Helen, but when she saw how distressed her friend looked, any doubts on this score disappeared. It was obvious that something terrible had happened – but was it really Graham, her husband, that Helen meant? How could something have happened to him? Where was he? How did Helen know something terrible had happened to Graham, if he was away on a business trip?

In reacting in this way, and asking these questions, Joyce was exactly following the first part of the pattern of realisation. Unable to take in the whole reality of what had happened, she had chosen a small part of it and tried to make sense of that. And the first step in making sense of it was to try to identify or define the bits of it that were really happening around her. The only bit that made sense at first was that Helen had arrived in a very distressed state having phoned to say something terrible had happened to Graham while he was away. She knew Helen had phoned and what Helen had said – she had experienced it for herself. So she clung to this as the only part she could really believe. Everything else – such as the reasons why Helen might have said such things – she rejected at first.

Identifying and defining

When we try to comprehend something that is extremely complex, some truth which is so momentous in its implications that it might change our whole life or force us to alter all we have believed up to now, we simply cannot do it all at once. So our minds start by identifying or defining one small part of it for us. We need to start from what we know to be true. So we pick out the bit that we have experienced directly with our senses.

We now have a small part of the total reality before us. It is this small part that we concentrate upon. We try to ignore the rest. If we can do this successfully, we can proceed towards some form of realisation. If, however, we find ourselves unable to ignore the rest, our concentration breaks down and we are overwhelmed again. We are back at square one, trying once more to identify or define a small part of the vast whole that we can think about clearly. This is how the task of accepting the full reality of what has happened begins.

31

The next stage

To describe the second part of the pattern, it will be helpful to return to Joyce – still trying to take in the news which Helen has given her. She began by accepting only the part that had happened directly to her. And she asked questions about identity – was it really her husband, her Graham, whom Helen was distressed about? Helen answered her questions. Graham had come to see her on his way home. He had felt very tired. He had gone upstairs to the bedroom to lie down. Later Helen had heard him shout, and he was having an attack of some sort. She had sent for the ambulance immediately. There had been nothing anybody could do. The hospital tried their best. He had died soon after they got him there.

Now Joyce began to accept that something terrible really had happened to Graham. She said later that at this point she felt more afraid than at any time in her life before. She and Helen clung to one another. For the first time since she heard the news Joyce cried. 'Then I felt angry with him,' she told me. 'I just knew he should not have gone on that bloody business trip.'

At this second stage of realisation, Joyce was no longer questioning the bit of the whole reality her mind had selected for her, but experiencing a massive attack on her sense of security. She had never felt so afraid. She felt angry, too. At the first stage she had been doubting, questioning what she knew. Now she knew that Graham had been hurt in some way, some way that was still too terrible to grasp. In her fear and her anger she wanted to turn on him and attack him. At this stage people often cry with frustration and rage, or angrily reject the news. It cannot be true, they say. It isn't fair – why should it happen to me? Why just now? How could he do that to me? There is no answer to these questions. They are not real questions, but a way of expressing the shattering sense of threat and insecurity which marks this stage of realisation. To cope with it, Joyce clung to Helen. At this stage we all reach out to find some means of assuaging our desperate need for safety.

Searching

When we physically cling to another person for security and reassurance, what is it that determines the moment when we let go? It is probably when both of us feel just about safe enough to separate and go within ourselves and face our feelings. Joyce and Helen clung to each other until they felt a little better, then Joyce became aware of her need to do something about her bewilderment and confusion. She did what she had grown used to doing over the many years of knowing Graham. She looked for him. 'Where is Graham?', she asked.

'He's in the hospital.'

'I must go to him,' said Joyce.

It was where she belonged, by his side, particularly if something really bad had happened to him. He would need her. She began to fetch her coat, but Helen restrained her. 'They won't let you see him yet,' she said.

The first stage of realisation had been *identifying* and *defining* the part of the total reality Joyce was trying to grasp, and she had tested this by doubting and questioning. At the second stage she had resolved enough doubt to face part of the desperate *insecurity* which the news about Graham had given her, and she had faced up to this part of the reality by crying and clinging. Now she felt a little less hurt she was able to think more realistically about Graham. It is typical of this third stage that she felt a need to be where she belonged, to exercise her dependency upon the person she most belonged to. This is often expressed by some form of *searching*. In Joyce's case, the small increase of certainty gained from clinging to Helen helped her understand how much more she needed Graham.

Joyce brushed aside what Helen had said, so Helen told her again. 'It's no good going to the hospital. There's nothing you can do. It's all over. They won't let you see him until tomorrow. At ten o'clock tomorrow.'

Assertion

'Of course they'll let me see him,' said Joyce. 'I'm his wife. They'll have to let me see him.' She was still trying to grasp that small bit of the total reality – that something terrible had happened to her husband. She belonged with him. But it was more than that. She was special to him and this special fact about her had to be asserted. The fourth stage of realisation always involves some kind of *assertion* reflecting the unique features of the person concerned.

She was now very close to realisation. Sensing this, Helen told her again that there would be nothing she could do, even if they let her see Graham. Not even she could help, even though she was Graham's wife. Joyce described this moment to me later as coming upon her 'like a thunderbolt'. She felt struck dumb. She realised that what had happened to her husband was something final, something far worse that she had believed possible.

Realising

Joyce had reached the goal her mind had set for her. She had accepted the unacceptable. The pattern of events during these very first moments of bereavement had gone through five stages – the same stages that occur with every act of realisation. In one sense, therefore, it is possible to say that at that moment she *realised* and *accepted* that her husband had died. But to say this would not be the whole truth. In fact, she had only accepted a very small part of what had happened.

Accepting the reality of loss means a great deal more than realising – and accepting the fact – that a person you love is so hurt that even you cannot help. Joyce still had not fully realised that Graham had died in the sense that she would never see him alive again, that he would never talk to her again, that he would never touch her again. There were, at that moment, many, many aspects of the loss of Graham which she did not have the resources to feel – let alone think about realistically.

Before we can accept or reject realistically what we think or feel might have happened to us, we need to complete the five stages of the process of realising. We need to live this experience for every aspect of the total reality. Over the next few chapters we will be looking at many examples of 'realisation' and how it works while we tackle the tasks of grief. How can we use this information about 'realising' to help ourselves do the work of grieving?

Trying too hard

There is an old motto, that if at first you do not succeed, then try, try, try again. When there is something you do not understand, something you want to realise but cannot quite grasp, it is often a good idea to keep trying. But not always. As with most things, the amount of effort you put into realising is not the key to success. Remember another motto – if at first you don't succeed, maybe you're trying too hard. Cudgelling your brains only makes you tired. You need to work at realising by using a modicum of technique, not just by a large expenditure of undirected energy.

So if you want to help yourself during the first weeks and months after bereavement it is important to remember the scale of the task. The full realisation of what has happened to you will not come all at once. It is far too big for that. But you can get there by small steps. Each step begins from what you know – either what you really feel or what you really think. If you are the sort of person who works things out best by talking to yourself, then do so in privacy, and have paper and pen handy so you can also write down key words. If, on the other hand, you are a very visual person, your thinking can be helped by drawing diagrams which represent the relationship between the things that puzzle you.

Many people are not so much verbal or visual thinkers as people who work things out above all by puzzling at them till they 'just feel right'. If you are like this you almost certainly need physical movement to help you try to realise things. You will know what works for you – a long walk in the fresh air, pacing up and down, exercises to help you relax. Whatever your normal style of thinking things through, use it, and make sure you have time and space to use it by planning your day to some extent. Stop when you feel tired, and have some other activity ready to go on to when you stop.

Your needs

You may be tempted to keep yourself too busy with little things so as to avoid thinking through the big ones. This happens to people partly because they are afraid, and partly because of anger. It is a form of worry that I call 'notting'.* It

* See *How to Cope with Your Nerves*, by the same author (Sheldon Press).

35

may be very difficult at times not to worry – but realisation will be slowed down by this. Part of the answer is to accept your own need to have unpleasant feelings, and the other part is to give in to them more often. When you are going through the business of realisation, each one of the five stages has it own associated feeling – a set of urges that you will experience. Let yourself feel these and express them as openly as you can. They are, in order of occurrence, doubting and questioning, rejecting and crying, searching and feeling lost, challenging your own specialness, and, finally, feeling that you have accepted something that used to scare you or make you feel angry.

You also need to tell other people about the way you feel. They can help just by listening and being there.

5

Facing Change

In the beginning it may be just about all you can do to understand that somebody very important to you is dead. It is hard to grasp what has happened to that person, and what has happened to you. In the ordinary way of things there will be people around almost all of the time for the first few days. Friends and relations will probably help as best they can. There will be a funeral. Then, quite suddenly, like most people, you find that you are on your own. The mourning is over for everybody else. You are left to get on with the rest of your life, to begin living with grief.

What are the realities that most people have to try to grasp during these next few weeks and months? How can they help themselves through this period? This is what we are going to look at next. First, we shall consider what it is you will probably begin to realise, and ways of dealing with the stress this will cause. We shall then look at the kind of crisis most of us go through at this time, and say a little more about how you can help yourself. After that, in the chapters that follow, we shall examine ways of resisting the isolation and dependence that can slow down your grieving and which is often the most lasting effect of grief.

Changed relationships

One of the first things people notice after somebody close to them has died is that bereavement alters relationships. This is true in several important ways. People you feel you have known for a very long time, for example, may treat you differently. Some of them seem distant, addressing you in formal sentences, standing further back when they talk to you, not staying so long when they visit but making excuses to leave early. They may suddenly become very conventional when you expected them to be their usual spontaneous selves. If you enjoy hearing the latest gossip about mutual friends from them you find that they are reluctant to pass this on, and when you challenge them, they say that surely you do not want to hear all that. It can take you a little while to realise that people

37

who do this are nervous of you and more than a little scared. Some of them are afraid you are going to make them feel miserable. Others are afraid you will have changed as a result of your bereavement, and that they will not be welcome any more.

There is often some substance in these fears. You might want to talk to them about how you feel when you are miserable, or tell them about some of the painful things that have happened. That, after all, is one of the things friends are for. But this can worry them. Also, some of the people you have hitherto thought of as your own friends were friends of both you and the person you have lost. Their relationship with you was not as close as it was with the person you are grieving for. They might feel that the main reason for being one of your friends has now gone. This often happens to wives whose main source of friends was their husband's place of work. The friends were really their husbands', rather than their own.

During the first few weeks, therefore, some of the people you thought of as your friends alter their behaviour towards you. At the same time, bereaved people often find that they are surprised at the help and support they receive from unexpected directions. Neighbours who had hardly spoken before turn out to be towers of strength. Acquaintances who you thought of as rather cold and dignified can surprise you by weeping with you and providing limitless warm, caring patience when you feel lost and unhappy or helpless and panicky.

I have often heard people say that when their husband or wife died, that is when they realised who their friends were. This is the kind of thing they meant. But unless you are actually going through this experience, it is hard to understand how painful and difficult it can be. First there are the doubts you will have about whether you have offended them or hurt them, or whether they really disliked you all along. After the doubting and questioning you begin to feel insecure with them – frustrated by their lack of informality, for example, or anxious for them since they seem so uncomfortable. If you are already holding back tears when they visit now, any insensitivity on their part can mean you find yourself weeping uncontrollably as soon as they have left. This second stage – rejecting and weeping from insecurity – gives way usually to a determination not to lose them as friends, a searching in your mind for common ground with them as you try to understand. You can only let go when you grasp the fact that they are not special to you any longer. Then the relief of accepting the fact that things have changed and that you really do not need to be hurt by this can flood over you, and you feel better.

The need to talk

Other relationships with the people around you are also likely to change. For example, if you lose your spouse, it can take you a little while to realise that some of the people who alter the way they treat you are now thinking of you as a single man or woman, even though you still think of yourself as married. Also, bereavement can effect your position in the power structure of your family. You may be expected by brothers and sisters to take over as head of the family, or to treat one of them as the new authority or mainstay. We shall look in more detail at some of these effects later, when we consider the impact on a family of loss of a parent.

But the most important relationship that has changed is that with the person who has died. Grieving is the continuation of this relationship by other means. You cannot simply switch it off as if it had never existed. You need to be able to talk about it.

The fun you used to have can be relived by reminiscing. The difficult times can be got into proportion far more accurately if you can recall them out loud in ordinary, natural conversation. Admitting feelings you have never told anybody about before at such times helps you to get across to other people a truer picture of yourself and the relationship you had with the person who has died. Above all you have to avoid harbouring hurts that you once protected as part of that living relationship which has now gone. Those hurts no longer have any real reason to stay alive – and dead hurts can fester. Talking them out in a natural way as part of everyday conversation with family or friends can not only help you feel better – it can also enable other people with similar experiences to talk them out too. You may be surprised how often the things you have hidden from other people turn out to be the kind of things they hid too. And how often you thought you had successfully concealed feelings from other people to avoid hurting them, when they knew about it all along and were not in the least bit upset.

A wall of silence

Unfortunately, your own need to talk can meet with the opposite effect. One of the least pleasant features of the way people deal with grief in our own culture is that there is often great reluctance to talk about the dead as they really were. There will, of course, be those superficial and embarrassed people who never mention the person you have lost once the funeral is over. They are hardly worth bothering about. But there is also the more subtle wall of silence that you can come up against when you try to be realistic about some of your mixed feelings towards the person you have lost.

Some of this is because the people around you disagree with you and do not want to hurt your feelings by saying so. In this they do you a disservice, since if they argued, maybe you would understand your own feelings better. Some of it is because what you are saying might force them to challenge their own assumptions about you, and this would lead to a loss of power on their part. We will look at examples of this later. But some of it is based on the superstition that it is dangerous to 'talk ill of the dead' – a superstition that has a long history in our culture, and goes back to the days when people believed that the air was filled with malevolent spirits that had to be appeased.

What takes many people a long time to realise when they meet a wall of silence, is that this is not their problem, but the problem of those who put up the wall. You will not make their difficulties worse by opening up your own feelings honestly. But if you fail to do so, you increase the risk of delay to your own grieving. Accepting the reality of your loss in respect of many aspects of your relationship can take longer unless you realise that other people's reluctance to do the same is a problem for them, not for you, to solve.

Talking with

In your private moments, you will probably discover what many have discovered before you – that it will help you to talk to the person you have lost as if he or she were still there. This is not something to be afraid of, or to feel ashamed about. It is not a sign that you are going mad. The relationship you had with that person is still there, and although it is changing, this need to feel that you are communicating will be part of you for a long time. Quite often your need to talk with the person you are missing can only be dealt with this way. If it helps you realise your need, it will have added another important section to your acceptance of what has happened. How can it help you realise?

Like all realisations this one will not come easily. You will probably find yourself questioning your need to talk, then try not to do it in case it would be wrong in some way. Next you will search for other ways of staying in touch with the person you are missing. You will probably search and fail, with the result that you go back to talking aloud with him or her, but still feel bad about it. Some people then decide that it is just one of their ways of being themselves – a special feature of their personality that they can simply accept and live with happily for the rest of their lives, always in private, and especially when they want to work out how they feel about important matters. The rest decide that their relationship with the dead person can still be special but does not need to be expressed this way. Their need to communicate is met in other ways or changes altogether. So they stop talking aloud to him or her.

Never the same again

During all these changes, the task that is before you is to accept that things will never be the same again. Your relationship with the person who died has altered irrevocably. Few of us can tackle this truth all at once. We have to approach it a few steps at a time. Some of these steps are extremely painful. For a great many of the people who grieve, they often lead to a fundamental crisis. We need next to see why this is so. We can then go on to look at why this crisis is so often the major

41

turning point which decides whether or not the person starts to emerge from the shadows towards a completed grieving.

The little things

When you have a living relationship with somebody you take little things for granted. Getting to know somebody, liking or loving that person, sharing a part of your life with him or her, all the big things we do with the people close to us are made up of thousands of small actions. Some of these actions happen inside you or inside the other person, as decisions or as feelings. But the fact that the relationship actually exists does not depend on these internal actions. It really exists because of the things that take place between you – the hundreds of thousands of small acts of communication that connect together what is going on inside each of you. Because of these multitudinous acts of communication, the things each of you thinks and feels are changed to take account of what the other person thinks and feels – and the relationship grows.

As long as the two of you are able to go on adding to this history of small acts of communication, you will both be part of a living relationship together. Some of our relationships stay alive with very little communication between us – as, for example, when friends seldom meet but still regard one another as friends. Other relationships generate a continuous daily stream of small additions to the history of what has gone on between us. This is usually what happens when we live with somebody and see them every day as part of our accepted way of life.

Many of the changes that will now take place are because the person you are missing is no longer there to make these small additions to your history as a couple. The fact that he or she is not there can be hard to accept. We saw earlier how the human mind breaks up a large truth into smaller sections, and then works on these so it can build up slowly towards a bigger realisation. This is what often happens when you try to realise that the person you most miss is really not there any longer and will never be there again.

Not there

How do you begin fully to realise that somebody is not there? One important part of the truth is that when you look round for the person, you cannot see him or her. At first this just gives you a feeling of puzzlement. Maybe you turn the corner as you come home, and find yourself expecting the person to be at home waiting for you. Maybe you walk into the next room because you thought you heard him or her. Maybe you are watching television, and glance towards his or her usual chair to exchange a smile about something you are enjoying. You expect to see the person, and you find yourself puzzled because you can't.

Your mind then takes the next step – the feeling of puzzlement gives way to one of insecurity. This could take the form of either fear, or anger, or worry. In the early days after bereavement, people find themselves gripped by panic at this point. Their mind rejects the reality, so they can only feel better by thinking the person will come back soon. But eventually they are able to get past this stage and start to feel less afraid. They still experience fear, or anger, or worry, but because this is less intense, and because they are learning not to reject the feeling, they can move to the next stage of realisation that he or she is not there.

This is the point at which you begin to recognise that the person cannot really be by your side. You search for the face but cannot find it. If this should happen, then you feel a dreadful sense of aloneness, a feeling of being lost and abandoned. This can defeat you too, so you cannot go further with the realisation, and relapse into impotent rage at the person for having left you like this, or a terrible fear that you will never survive by yourself. But if it does not defeat you, and you are able to get through the feeling to the other side, you are able to have confidence in your own special qualities – that you have survived before, that you have enough courage, enough resources to get through this time. Then, if you can do this, you will find yourself accepting that he or she is not there, and you will have won for yourself a small part of the total reality of your loss.

Time

It is sometimes said that time heals. If this is true, it does not do its work automatically. The passage of time is no guarantee by itself that the intensity of your feelings will lessen. But as time goes by you have more practice at living with feelings which accompany realisation. Your mind slowly becomes accustomed to living with the facts.

Time gives you opportunities to realise other aspects of the fact that he of she is not there any longer. It is not just that you cannot see the person. You cannot hear that familiar voice again, except in your own head. The chance over-hearing of one very like it can trigger a realisation with all the painful feelings you had avoided flooding over you once more. Or you will find yourself doing something you would in the old days have told him or her about, and go through – or fail at – the process of realising that you will never again see and hear the reactions which for so long were a living part of your life.

And when you talk about the person, having carefully schooled yourself at first to use the past tense – to say 'she was' or 'he would have been' instead of 'she is' or 'he will be' – you will forget at times and withdraw into yourself, puzzled, then identify what you have said, be assailed by insecurity, search for the truth, know that things are different now, and accept that the past tense is the right one to use.

Time brings practice. It is the trying to realise and the succeeding that give time its therapeutic quality in grief. If healing takes place then it is not because the work of realising grows less as time passes. It is because you get better at it, so each small realisation takes less time to accomplish. Each little step is stumbled over at first. The times you miss him or her most – bed-time, meals, coming home to a now enpty house, shopping just for yourself, the sight of clothes in a wardrobe or a pair of his or her worn shoes – these little, taken-for-granted things lie like mines in a minefield to explode your hard-worn composure.

Refusal to accept

We cannot always succeed. There are going to be times when the failures become too great to bear. Accepting that things will never be the same again feels at times to be an impossible task. The small crises accumulate into a large one. How do you face this crisis? What can you do when your whole being refuses to accept reality?

6

Crisis

To feel tired is one thing. To feel totally exhausted from almost superhuman efforts to achieve the impossible is quite a different feeling. It can come upon you suddenly, in the midst of completing some trivial task, something you have done a thousand times before – a routine procedure at your place of work, a simple domestic chore like ironing or washing up. Or the feeling can grow by inches over a day or so, until one day it is too big to be ignored. Your mind clears. You feel laid waste with exhaustion, but you see the truth in all its detail, like something perfectly illuminated in a brilliant photograph. You know that you are wasting your time. You simply cannot go on any more. It is all over. There is no point in trying any longer.

There have probably been other kinds of crisis – the kind, for example, where you cry yourself to sleep in the hope that you will never wake up, or the kind where you suddenly want to step in front of the heavy lorry that is hurtling towards you, jump in front of the train you have waited to catch, or drive your car off the road and into that steep river valley where it will be smashed to pieces. But this is different. You are not feeling impulsive. You have never felt more sane. But the fact remains that you have reached the end. You are tired out.

This is the true crisis of grief. Before, death offered itself to you irrationally, and although you could have taken that death by one small-seeming step, you were not ready. Now you are ready, and rational enough to plan. You believe that you are at last accepting reality, that when you thought you could survive you were merely following some kind of delusion. How have you reached this conviction, and what are you going to do about it?

Cannot change — will not change

We must begin by recognising the truth. The person you want to have alive and by your side will never be alive and by your side again. Nothing you can do will change that. At first you tried to alter this fact. You acted as if he or she would be back

46

one day. Then you began to accept that this was not possible. So you concentrated on the various changes you were faced with.

But some things you decided you would never change. You could not bear these things to alter. This is because you, yourself, the fundamental things about you and the way you live, the things you have always stood for, the things that make you different, the things that properly belong to you, the way you are – this is what is now being challenged. All that is being steadily eroded, or being dramatically forced to alter. And you cannot do it. It is too much to ask of anyone, and now you can see that more clearly than ever before.

If you give in to these changes it seems you will be turning your back on everything that matters. Yet there seems to be no choice – to go on living will mean altering irrevocably all that you value in life, and losing it all for ever. The only rational answer, since you cannot change the facts, is to end your own life.

Your choice

There is another side to this truth, or rather another layer of truth beneath this one. Your choice is between living and dying. That is nobody else's business but yours. People will probably disagree about this – they will argue that your life also belongs to other people, to your family if you have one, to the community at large if you have no family. Maybe it does in part belong to them, but they do not seem to want it as it is, or you would not be feeling this way. The fundamental decision as to whether you live or die cannot be left to them. It is your life, and only you can do with it what you want to – including end it.

Some people will point out that although it is your life, you will be behaving irresponsibly if you end it. People depend on you – at work, at home, in the neighbourhood. Even if this is not true, they argue, you should spare a thought for the poor devils who have to clear up the mess after you have killed yourself. But this is a fatuous argument when you really look at it. It would be silly to equate the momentary inconvenience they would suffer from, and soon recover from, with the endless desperation of a seemingly pointless life that would be facing you if you let your courage fail you now.

What then is this other layer of truth you might have missed? It is simple, and we have already said it. You have the choice. It is, possibly for the first time in your life, *your* life. You never asked for it. You were not consulted about your own conception. Up to now you have led the life which, very largely, others have given you. Now it is yours. You are its sole arbiter. And this fact in itself is very important.

Irony

For days now, perhaps for many weeks, you have battled on. But the tug of war which you have been subjected to deep in your mind comes to an end when you realise that you can actually face the thought of killing yourself. You feel more at peace with yourself than you have felt for a long time. At the moment of defeat, the spoils of victory are yours.

You have at last achieved control over the most important thing you have – your own life. And you want to destroy it. You have one power left – the power of death. Opposing that power is love – love of life, love of yourself. They are old enemies, these two, power and love. Now they are fighting over you again – this time, out in the open where you can see them. On whose side will you fight?

You are at the centre of the crisis. You have to make a commitment one way or the other. You are tired, but calm. And you are alone in a way you have never had to face before. If there is enough love in you, then you will need all your last reserves of courage, but you will commit yourself to life. If there is more power than love, you will plan your death, and try to accomplish it. But if there is neither enough love of life, nor enough power in you, enough energy or courage to end that life, then you will live on, but with a lesser, and enfeebled commitment to life. You will let a part of you die, without adding to the part of you that lives. Will you accept life, reject it, or dodge the issue?

Emerging

Although you may not realise this at the time, none of these decisions can be a final one. If your courage fails, and you try

48

to end your life but cannot bring yourself to do so, then you will recover from the hurt this causes you, but you will also have deferred the decision until later. You will run the risk of having to face it again sooner or later. And if you decide to die, then you have other decisions to make – practical ones about how you will do it.

I suspect that those who do succeed in killing themselves do so mainly by default, rather than by decision. I don't really know. The final decision to die seems to me to require something other than a true decision – perhaps a decision not so much to die as to let something kill you, and to increase the risk of this happening.

What I do know, as well as I know anything else, is that if you take a positive decision to live, if you accept the need to go on whatever the consequences, you emerge from the crisis stronger than you went into it. That may not be very strong. But you will be free from some of the death that has been trying to take over your life. If you take no positive decision, neither increasing your commitment to life nor increasing your commitment to death, and let the exhaustion you feel have its way, you will eventually sleep, and maybe feel better when you wake. And, if you want to, you can do this for a very long time – spending your reserves of energy as fast as you collect them by putting off for years the decision as to who or what controls whether you live or die. Somebody else's death, acting through the intermediary of your grief, will be blackmailing you – always demanding payment, and never being satisfied.

And if you increase your commitment to life, what then? You know that you can change your mind, and that henceforth you are living because you want to – not because other people made you do it, or talked you into it, or stopped you killing yourself, or because you did not have the courage to do anything else. It takes courage to live. It always will. It takes the courage to be imperfect, to fail, to accept the responsibilities of imperfection and failure. Living without courage is easy when this is somebody else's reponsibility. When it is your decision it is you who have to pay for it. You emerge from the crisis knowing this. All the problems you had before are still waiting for you. *Now they have to be faced.*

Living with loss

Things around you have been changing since your bereavement. You have accepted some changes, but until the crisis you have not sufficiently faced up to your own need to change. As you emerge from crisis, you are able at last to see with new eyes what you have lost. Before, you did not want to look 'too' closely.

The extent of your loss as a person has to be subject to that familiar process of realisation. Until this is done it will not be a real loss, but a fantasy loss – something that exists only as a set of imagined probabilities in your own head. It will not bear close examination – and this is what people mean when they say 'it does not bear thinking about' or 'I dare not go into that too deeply'. If you accept your loss as real, and accept the need to go on, then you can examine in detail what that loss is, and learn to be fully alive again, rather than only partly alive.

Realising the loss

Let us use the process of realisation, and apply it together to what you have lost. What will we have to do? First we will need to define the area we can tackle – and this will mean going through the feelings of *doubting* and *questioning*. If you get through these feelings, we will be able to move on to the next stage, which is to look at your own loss of *security* – not just money, of course, but security in every sense of the word. You may be prone to reject my ideas at this stage – to say they do not apply in your case, to want to stop reading, or skip ahead. You might feel that you have to force yourself to read on. Or you might wonder what all the fuss is about, since you feel nothing very much either way. Any of these reactions might be a response to fear or anger or worry, or they might not be. I guarantee nothing. You will have to decide for yourself.

The third stage will be to look at your loss of '*belonging*' – to examine what you have lost in terms of what was your very own. It will hurt you again if you can really get in touch with it. But it will not harm you unless you let it. If you can feel your sense of loss, however, and stay with it, you will also be able to give up some of the need to feel lost as a person. When you

50

have done this, we can move to the fourth stage – which will be about your own *specialness*. We will by then be in a position – if you want to be – to look at the extent to which you are no longer special because of what you have lost. The fifth stage is even more up to you than the earlier ones – it is to accept or to reject the idea that you have changed as a result of your loss.

A word of caution is in order at this point. If you have not read the earlier part of this book before looking at this page, then the rest of this chapter may be quite meaningless to you.

How Have You Changed?

How have you changed since your bereavement? That is the question you need to focus on first. See if you can answer systematically. You may have changed physically. Some people, for example, lose weight or put on weight. This may go back to before the bereavement, and due to the worry caused by the situation that led up to the bereavement. If so, then it is part of grieving. Weight change is significant if it means you have neglected your health or your appearance in response to what has been happening to you. Have there been other physical changes? Has your appearance altered at all? Are you less well? Has there been a recurrence or worsening of some earlier medical problem, or the appearance of a new one? And what about your sexual feelings? Have these stayed the same as they were, increased, or become less intense or less frequent?

Next, think about behavioural change. Has your behaviour altered? Do you think you treat people in general differently – or any one person in particular? Who? For example, is your work suffering? Is it harder now for you to remember things or concentrate on things that used to absorb you? More important than this, do you feel less confident or less clever now you do not have the person you miss by your side? In what ways? If you think back to the value of your own experience, how has this changed? Is it still the same, or will it never feel the same again.

Now turn to the question of money and property. What has altered here? Have there been changes? Do you have less money or the same or more money? Do you still own the material objects that you owned before, or have you lost some of them, or gained more? The significant point, however, is – how do you feel about this? Do these things matter in exactly the same way they used to? Or has it changed? Are they more important to you, or less important? Try not to make moral judgements – whether they ought to matter more or matter less – just concentrate on defining whether or not there has been a change.

The last set of questions is about you as a social being. Do you take less, more, or the same interest in having and making friends? Do you put the same effort into keeping in touch with friends, family, and neighbours, or has this changed? If so, precisely how? Do you take the same interest in the world at large that you used to, in sport or current affairs? How has your interest changed, if at all?

It is now up to you to use the above list to try to identify any changes in you as a person as a result of what has happened to you. Ask yourself how you have altered, precisely, if you can. Try to pin down any doubts you have about whether you are still the same person you used to be.

How do you feel?

When you think about these changes, maybe you will feel that they are all acceptable. None of them is causing you any real problem. You are not angry about them, worried about them, or anxious about them. If so, then you can stop grieving right now, or start being honest with yourself. But be quite sure before you do either of these things that you are not hiding anything from yourself. One clue will be if your response to the question – do any of these changes make you feel angry or afraid or worried – is 'not really'. This means 'yes – a little bit!' What is that little bit? Is it really only a little bit? Or is it quite a lot, really?

Now think about that feeling. What is it that makes you angry or afraid or worried? It could be one of a number of things. You did not deserve what happened to you. It was unfair. The future is now uncertain. You cannot get through the next few days, and this worries you because you are angry and afraid. People now expect too much of you. You will never be able to love anybody again, or to trust anybody ever again. You would run away if there was somewhere to go. You want to wake up and find that none of it ever happened.

Now ask yourself this question. Whoever it is who might be to blame for the way you feel, who is *responsible* for the way you feel? I am going to suggest to you that you are responsible. You are in charge of your own feelings. This is not intended to be a moral judgement, but a plain statement of fact. If you want to reject this fact, then you can. It might mean going back into the crisis to find out for yourself all over again whether you want to accept life or not. But the fact that you are angry or afraid is your problem. Only you can solve it. It is no use blaming that on the person who died. Your crisis may be no more than a very dramatic and very dangerous grown-up temper tantrum. If that is what it is, then recognise the fact. You are entitled to have it. You might as well enjoy it. But when it is all over, what are you going to do? And if it isn't a temper tantrum, but something far worse, then you need to face up to that too. If you need money, tell somebody and get the help you need. If there are other practical ways you can be helped, then get your tantrum or your panic over with, and go and ask the people who can give you the help you need.

Sense of loss

It is time to let go of your sense of loss. That sense of loss will only fall away if you can see that you are not fundamentally damaged inside by what has happened. Maybe you have changed. You have lost things you value, things which nobody else had, things which made you unique and special. You will never have precisely those things again. Does this make your life not worth living? Were you fundamentally more valuable inside before the bereavement than you are now, after it? If you were unique and special before, then all that has happened can only make you more unique and special. It has not happened to anybody else in quite this way. It surely makes you more, not less special. If you were not unique before, then I don't believe you.

Hope

Maybe you will never meet anybody who will mean the same to you as the person you have lost – it is unlikely that you will.

Each person who dies leaves a gap that is never filled in quite the same way, if it is filled at all. And since time began, people have been forced to change as a result. We can resist that force, or we can accept it. What you do and how you do it is up to you. But although it's none of my business, I hope you will accept life, and learn all over again the wisdom and the beauty of staying alive and loving.

7

Resisting Isolation

Isolation from other people is one of the most damaging, and most lasting effects of bereavement. It can take many forms. The most obvious is when bereavement leaves you in a house by yourself, with no family or friends, and no neighbours for miles around. But even with family around you – husband, or wife, or children – and with many close friends who are concerned about you, you can suffer from isolation.

This may be because you feel a need to withdraw from people, to hold back from close contact when they do not understand or appreciate your special grief. There are also families which reject the grieving person, using him or her as a scapegoat for their own bad feelings.

For most of us, isolation from other people has the effect of reducing our quality of life. We need people around us. When we are isolated we begin to lose touch with the reality of who we are, what our place is in the world, and whether that place is worth having. We retreat into fantasy. Our actions seem strange to others, because we are reacting to our imagined version of what is happening, not to the truths which other people can see around them, and which we do not want to see or have forgotten how to see.

An important part of the work of grieving, therefore, is to *resist* isolation in all its forms. To do this we need first to understand it. Being physically isolated from people means having varying degrees of distance between you and somebody else. How does this happen, and what can you do about it?

Severe isolation

It will be helpful to begin by looking at some examples of severe isolation. Joan, for example, is a woman who wrote to me after a broadcast about loneliness. She and her husband had planned for a long time to move away from the suburbs when he retired, and buy a pretty bungalow at the seaside. Their children were grown up, and, wrote Joan, 'didn't need us any longer'. All went according to plan at first. Her husband retired, they found a place and moved in, and although they did not manage to make friendly contact with neighbours, they were 'reasonably happy'. Weekend visits from the children and grandchildren were frequent at first, even though the little ones were fractious when they got there after the long journey. But after a time these became rarer, and Joan felt the excuses were a tiny bit flimsy. Then, sixteen months after they had moved in, Joan's husband had a stroke and, a few days later, he died.

It will be a familiar story to many people. Joan was left isolated in a bungalow miles away from the people she had spent most of her life with – her friends and neighbours back in the suburbs. Her children and grandchildren were also inaccessible. Joan did not have the means to go to see them from time to time on impulse, and they were living their own lives with no real place for her in any case. They asked her 'as a matter of course, but not really meaning it' to move in with one of them, but she was understandably very much against this. Her neighbours remained aloof. She had nobody she could talk to about her grief. She was severely isolated, and felt herself 'going downhill'.

Marie's story was similar, except that her husband died before retirement. The plans had been made a long time before, and she had been looking forward to moving to the seaside as much as he had. So she went alone. Her two grown-up sons took turns to help her move and settle in, and then left her to it. She began to try to live the life which she and her husband had planned. When she wrote to me, Marie had been there nearly two years, and was 'trying to stay cheerful'. She was attending evening classes to try to meet people, and had broken the habit of a lifetime to become a pub regular. But she 'now realised that she had to live her own life'. She had moved there because in her grief for her husband, she had tried to 'do it for both of them'. It had been a mistake. 'I hope you'll tell people not to make the same mistake,' she added.

This kind of severe geographical isolation from people you care about makes the work of grieving very much harder. Not only is there nobody around you with whom you can share memories of the person you have lost, but there are often reasons for the move away from family and friends which were not closely examined and dealt with as part of the relationship before bereavement. Joan, for instance, would not be un-typical if the majority of reasons she had for moving came from a need to please her husband, rather than from pleasing herself.

Many of the Joans who are isolated in this way hide their resentment at such a move, or have it ignored by their husbands, but can only control the anger inside them while their husbands are alive. Such a problem can go back many years, and be tolerated by the victim for a variety of reasons. If he or she is to complete the work of grieving, then these hidden feelings have to be dealt with. They need to be talked about, got into proportion, and acted upon in some way. Otherwise the grief will be bottled up and delayed, perhaps for ever, and there will be only a facade of grief covering up resentment and growing bitterness. The pretty coasts of Europe and North America are inhabited by quite a high proportion of people who live as resentful and unapproachable permanent memorials to the undefeated power of the browbeating husbands and bullying wives who took them there, and died.

A Lifeline

It has to be said, too, that if you find yourself in the same situation as Joan or Marie, and you do not want to end as an embittered lonely old man or woman, help is not at all easy to obtain. Most of us are frightened at the prospect of becoming a burden to our children. We are often not sure how to talk to them. Some of us dread turning into an interfering nuisance to them; others rightly suspect that we will have to put up with the nuisance created by their interference in our lives. In practical terms, neither we nor they may have the money for appropriate re-housing – the quaintly named 'Granny flat' from which an elderly person can come and go as he or she pleases, but still pop in to see children and grandchildren more or less on impulse.

Yet some kind of lifeline is needed, either from private individuals, collectives such as voluntary organisations in the neighbourhood, or from the community in the form of state sponsored help. You may have to choose the lesser of two evils – being a 'burden' to your family, or accepting help from strangers. Whichever you choose, it may help you to remember that you are worth a lot of trouble. A lot of years have gone into making you who you are, and all that you know is worth knowing. If you resist isolation, keep yourself really alive, and accept the need for help, you will immeasurably increase your chances not only of being less of a burden, but also of enriching the world we all share with you.

Remember also that there is no resistance without conflict. You cannot succeed unless you are prepared to challenge the fixed ideas other people have about you, and either get them to change these or, failing this, get your own way in spite of them.

Psychological isolation

Some people who are isolated are surrounded by people who know them. This is what happened to a woman I shall call Brenda, when her mother died. Brenda was in her thirties then, married, with two children under ten, and living with her husband. She had several aunts, uncles, and cousins in the neighbourhood, and an elder sister lived in a town only a few miles away. Her father had died some years earlier, and Brenda and her mother were described by her husband as 'getting on well enough together, though not particularly close'. I met them as a couple when they decided to look for help because of sexual difficulties. The problem seemed to both of them to date back to the death of Brenda's mother.

It turned out to be a complicated story. The main point, however, was that Brenda, after almost a lifetime of discord between her and her mother, had, in the last few months of her mother's life, developed a new kind of relationship with her. She had resented what she saw as the way the rest of the family neglected her mother, and since she also felt neglected, this had apparently brought them closer together. Brenda had said nothing about this to the rest of the family at the time, except her husband. He had been mildly interested but no more than that, and she recalled later that he had insisted that she must not neglect her household chores to spend time with her mother. The funeral had been a grand affair, not at all what Brenda knew her mother wanted. After that there had been what Brenda described as a 'greedy and undignified quarrel' over the money and the house her mother left.

Brenda had not cried at the funeral, nor since. If they noticed, the other members of the family probably assumed that this was just a reflection of the 'fact' that Brenda had never got on with her mother.

Brenda now became isolated. She no longer spoke to her extended family more than she had to out of politeness. Communication began to grow worse between her and her husband. 'She wouldn't let me touch her,' he said. She still played with the children and cuddled them, but she withdrew from everybody else, so that all they had of her were rather distant and grudging encounters. He then did the worst thing possible under the circumstances – he 'tried everything'. This means he pretended to like her so he could plead with her, and when this did not work he hit her, and when this did not work he told her to see a psychiatrist, and when she refused to go alone, he said he loved her and that he couldn't live with her any longer, and was leaving.

What emerged later was that Brenda had felt isolated by the family long before her mother died, and that after the funeral she had been so angry that instead of accepting this passively she had 'helped it along' – that is to say, she had taken over what she saw as the family's policy towards her and carried it out even more thoroughly than they had. This way, she felt, they would have to acknowledge eventually that they had all been wrong about her. The isolation she had felt at the time of her bereavement – even if she had not acted the way she did – would have slowed down her grieving. Her attempts to resist afterwards had been thwarted by the family's inability to notice her changed relationship with her mother. So she had forced all the hidden feelings out into the open, rather than be treated by everyone else as less than a person in her own right.

Risking conflict

Brenda's story is perhaps an extreme example of the way people can open up conflict when they resist isolation. Or perhaps it is merely that in her case the conflict was partly of her own making, and other people would have backed down earlier than she did. In many respects, however, it is no less a familiar story to many of us than that of Joan. We cannot ignore the power of the family if we are to understand in general the difficulties people face in resisting isolation. Yet if they are to do the work of grieving, isolation must be resisted.

Brenda's method of withdrawing was to increase the 'distance' between her and the rest of her family with the exception of the children. This means that her ways of communicating became more formal, more like those of a stranger. In effect, she withdrew her love, and used her power. She no longer talked with them, she talked at them. She detached herself from her husband in the sense that she no longer took part in mutual behaviour with him – rejecting his touch, for example. She became separate from him without leaving the house or his bed. She restricted herself to doing duties, and stopped giving and sharing with him. Whatever the rights or wrongs of what he did and what she did, the only answer in the end to such withdrawal is to recognise that it is a use of power. She could be broken by the use of more power, or won over by being loved enough to feel she could trust people again. In the event, Brenda and her husband took a long time to recognise this, and then made a successful fresh start by moving away from the extended family. Both eventually recognised one another's need to grieve. Both recognised how much more they had to learn about love.

Risking conflict – whether you do it Brenda's way or in a less extreme way – is a way of testing those around you. Do they really love you, accept you as a real person in your own right, or are you only acceptable as long as you continue to behave as an object they can manipulate?

An object lesson

When Derek's father died, Derek's mother came to stay for a few weeks. Sonja, Derek's wife, and their three teenage children were, like Derek, very fond of his mother, but a little anxious about how things would work out. The idea was that if all went well, they would try to persuade Derek's mother to move into a house nearby. They began by making a great fuss of 'Gran' – cups of tea in bed in the morning, running her everywhere in the car. 'Gran' became increasingly irritated, which at first Derek and Sonja put down to reaction to the bereavement. They overrode her protests, telling her that 'of course she wanted to go in the car – it was no trouble', and 'of course she had to go to bed now, she must be tired'. She was allowed to do little chores because 'it was good for her', but she only grew more and more withdrawn. Derek and Sonja were worried.

One day Sonja found her in the bedroom, her eyes damp, packing her suitcase. Sonja felt very distressed and hovered in the doorway. 'What's the matter, Gran,' she asked. Gran turned on her. 'I know you've tried to be very kind,' she said, 'but I'm not "Gran" – my name is Betty. I'm a woman called Betty. I'll stay if I can be Betty, but otherwise I'm leaving.' Sonja went over to her and put her arms around her. The two women wept together. Over the next few days they worked out what had gone wrong. 'Gran' had been treated like some very precious object – not as the person she was. Uncertain how to express love for her, they had used power instead. The fact that they had used it to protect her had not altered this fact. But by resisting this, Betty had been able to bring a new realism into her life and theirs, and to be loved for what she was, not for what they had mistakenly thought she was.

Retreat

Military generals are fond of saying that there is no such thing as retreat – only withdrawal in strength. But for some grieving people, those who do not have the resources to stand against the power applied to them to make them conform, those who cannot obtain access to real love and be treated as people in their own right, there is no other option available but retreat.

The most common form this takes is illness – either the giving-in to chronic stress symptoms such as back-pain, palpitations, or tight-chestedness, or the emergence of new symptoms, such as insomnia or hypertension. Any one of these symptoms must be taken seriously for its possible medical significance. The pain they cause will be real pain, the distress felt is real distress. But at the same time, it should be recognised that in a grieving person they are also a frequently encountered and always justified cry for help. The trouble so often is that they are seen only in strictly medical terms – possibly because doctors so often are people who lack the training, or experience, or the motivation to look beyond this, and to know what to do.

8

Resisting Dependence

Many of the problems which people begin to tackle as part of their grieving have been with them for a long time. But before bereavement they were either unable or unwilling to do something about them, or unaware that the problem existed. Many people, for example, are often unaware of how uncommitted they are to life until they are forced to face up to this by going through a major crisis. Relationship difficulties, such as suppressed feelings of bitterness or frustration, may have caused major communication breakdown in a marriage. But for various reasons these are not dealt with while both partners are alive. After the bereavement the feelings are much harder to suppress, and the person can either face up to them or bottle them up again and risk being unable to grieve completely. The need for help is also present in many cases long before bereavement forces the grief-stricken person to ask for help or to accept it.

One major problem which is a part of almost every grief is that of dependence. We are more likely to miss those people whom we most needed. And the more we needed a person, the greater the likelihood that we depended on him or her in some way. Living with grief means living with this problem, and eventually solving it. So the next step we need to take is to look carefully at the whole issue of dependence and independence.

What is dependence?

Dependence is what happens when something you need, and cannot obtain for yourself, is supplied by somebody else. Perhaps the most obvious example is financial dependence. In our culture, most wives with young children either do not go out to work, or cannot earn as much as their husbands. The standard of living they have as a family depends on the husband's income. Losing this income will mean that the need for money becomes acute. If they already have a very low standard of living, there may not be enough for basic things like food, warm clothing, or housing. Even if their standard of

62

living was quite high before the loss of the husband's income, there will still be many problems.

Loss of a husband's income can happen in several ways. It may be due to loss of a job, to illness which prevents him from continuing full-time work, or it may be a result of bereavement. Any of these usually has a direct impact on the standard of living of the family by threatening or even destroying their ability to maintain it.

There are two important points to take note of here, if we are to understand what dependence is. The first point is that we are never just 'dependent' – we are 'dependent for' something. So far, we have only mentioned money. But there are many other things we can be dependent on somebody for – and we shall need to look at the most important of these, including being dependent on somebody for love and affection. The second point is that the impact which loss has on us is relative. That is to say, it doesn't ultimately matter whether a family was rich or poor before the income was lost – both are faced with disaster and both are likely to be equally terrified or hurt. We experience the loss because the standard of living we are used to is threatened – whatever that standard might be.

For example, a child who has to be told that he cannot go on a school camp he has been looking forward to all term, is just as likely to be upset by this – perhaps even more upset – as one who is told that although his shoes let water in, he cannot have any new ones for a very long time if at all. The absolute loss in the second case may be greater, but the feelings created by the loss – in both cases – depend not on this, but on how much they were looking forward to what they have lost.

Not just the money

If we only depended on somebody for the money he or she supplied before we lost that person, then how much damage we suffered would depend on how much we relied upon having their money. But that would be all we would lose – just the money. We might be very upset, and suffer a great deal from the lowering of our standard of living, but we would be grieving for the money, not for the person.

Usually when we grieve for a person, we have lost things we

value at least as much as money. Loss of money can threaten our 'standard of living', but loss of these other things will threaten our 'standard of life'. As a result of this loss we may feel, for example, that we may never be loved again, may never be regarded as attractive again, may never again have somebody who trusts us or encourages us, takes care of us, or truly understands us. From now it may be simply impossible to go on being the person we are used to being, because we depended on somebody else for the means – whatever those happened to be – to go on being that person.

The more you depended on somebody so you could be yourself, the harder it will be to manage without him or her. And the threat to your standard of life is relative – not absolute. The husband who is lost may not have been the most reliable, the most faithful, the cleverest and most successful man in the world, but if you needed him around so your own life made sense then none of this matters. What matters is how much your standard of life – the extent to which you were able to get the things out of life which you expected, which you felt made life worth living – depended on having him around.

Grief is harder if you were dependent

Clearly we grieve the least for those who either meant nothing to us because they had no effect at all on our personal way of life, or for those who seemed determined to prevent us from achieving the minimum standard of life we felt we were entitled to. We may still grieve for such people, but not as much as for those on whom we depended to a very large degree. But that is not the only connection between grieving and dependence. It is also important to recognise that the more we grieve for somebody and the harder it is to get over that grief – the more dependent we must have been on the person who has died. In other words, those who find it hardest to complete the tasks of grieving are the people whose dependence on the person they have lost was so great that they cannot, even now, be themselves without that person.

They will find it harder to accept the reality of their loss, since this reality is more threatening to them. They will have more difficulty in accepting the need to go on, since their need to change is greater. They are likely to need more help because of this too. And resisting isolation becomes much more of a problem if you feel that what you have lost is something irreplaceable, that nobody else could possibly understand.

Immediately after a bereavement, people are just as dependent on the person they have lost as they were when he or she was alive. It would be strange if they were not, since the only thing that has altered is that he or she is no longer alive. Nothing else has had time to change or to be changed. But over the next few days, the next weeks and months, the person who has died cannot meet the needs of those left behind. It is then that the grieving person begins to realise the extent to which he or she depended on him or her. This may not have been realised before.

Finding out

It is sometimes said that you don't know what you have lost until you try to do without it. There is some truth in this, but it is not the whole truth. Certainly the extent to which you have depended upon somebody starts to become much clearer when you try to manage without that person. For example, even an apparently trivial problem like replacing a broken light bulb can become a relatively major one for somebody who has never done this before, or who is used to being told that he or she is no good at such tasks and always does them the wrong way. More difficult tasks which the person we depended upon used to do for us can seem totally beyond us when we first try to do them for ourselves. We have to face many of them without anybody to show us what to do or tell us whether we are tackling them the right way. At such times we can become painfully aware of the fact that we miss the person who used to do these things for us.

But this only takes us part of the way towards finding out exactly how much we depended on the person we have lost. At first all it shows us is that something we wanted to do for ourselves is harder than we thought. We can very easily miss the connection between this and still being dependent. For example, not being able to fix a light bulb, do the shopping, repair a broken fence – all the small, practical things we might have been used to somebody else doing for us – may be something we explain to ourselves by saying we are not very good at such things. And this is even more likely with larger, more complicated issues like selling a house, handling pension or insurance problems, dealing with the authorities over taxes and so on. Here we tend to accept that we cannot do such things, and ask somebody else for help. We transfer our dependence from the person we have lost to somebody else, and since we expect to be dependent we are even less likely to question this and wonder why we are not independent.

Trying to be independent and learning from your mistakes will certainly help you to recognise some of the ways you have been dependent on the person you have lost, but it is not enough to give you the whole picture. The danger is that you might blame your mistakes on yourself and underestimate your dependence, or get somebody else to help you and accept your lack of independence instead of questioning it. The first step in realising is to identify and define the problem, and the second one is to face up to the insecurity the problem creates. You might easily miss the first step because the person you depended on for so long actively encouraged you to avoid this insecurity so you would become even more dependent.

Vested interest

What is so often not understood is that within a great many of our everyday relationships, it is considered normal and acceptable for one person to set out consciously and deliberately to make the other one dependent on him or her. Failure to make somebody dependent is often regarded as a sign of inadequacy. For example, it is considered to be a husband's duty almost universally in our culture to be able to 'support' his wife. In effect, this means earning so much more than she could that there would be no point in her 'working' independently. Instead she becomes a housewife, dependent upon his superior earning power, works equally hard or even harder, but is not paid. There are signs that this traditional system is less widely accepted than it used to be a generation ago, but it still applies to most marriages even when those with dependent children are not counted. Men who earn less than their wives are regarded as unusual – even inadequate.

66

Many men, or course, have a vested interest in this system. It helps them to feel strong and protective and 'manly' to have somebody dependent upon them. It shows 'that they care'. Many women also benefit to some extent because they subscribe to the same view and would not want their men to feel inadequate. Few of them benefit by having less work to do, because if they have young children or a part-time job they are usually expected to make sure these activities do not lessen the amount of work done directly for their husbands or in keeping the home clean and tidy so he can be free from all but the simplest domestic chores.

Not only is a man's 'failure' to acquire and maintain a dependent woman regarded widely as a sign of inadequacy, a woman's 'failure' to acquire a man to depend on is also regarded with suspicion. Unmarried women over thirty with no attached male tend to find themselves treated as a threat by most married women, and as fair game for sexual harassment by a large number of attached males. They are also likely to be suspected of sexual deviance if they object. Being a divorced mother of young children is no protection either. The 'crime' is failure to be dependent on a male – not being unmarried.

Display

Dependence in our everyday relationships goes far deeper than all this, of course. We seldom question, for example, the way in which most of us set out to make our most significant sexual relationships exclusive. The majority of us try to make our partners depend entirely on us for sexual satisfaction, by convincing them that for the rest of their lives nobody will ever love them as much as we do, nor make love to them as well as we do. We want them to feel that nobody else could find them as attractive as we do – in effect, that everybody else finds them relatively unattractive.

On public occasions partners carefully control one another's displays of sexuality – husbands veto dresses that are 'too sexy' and wives put a stop to any advances husbands might make to other women. Dependence is carefully underlined by such methods as telling funny stories about recent incidents in which some simple task was messed up by one partner – or would have been but for the superior skill of the other partner. Men are supposed to eat out of tins while their wives are away, and women to be incapable of simple tasks like fitting a plug to electrical apparatus. Perhaps it is all harmless, meaningless fun. Yet the need for it is real enough. It helps people feel good to have somebody privately dependent and publicly displayed as dependent.

This need for dependence is not confined to adult sexual and marital relationships. Parents often regard it as their duty to restrict the development in their children of independent thought and action. Throughout the West it is more normal for parents to discourage, than to encourage, their adolescent children to experiment sexually, or to become active members of political and religious organisations to which the parents are opposed. Throughout a child's life its parents will probably reserve the right to question any major decision its child may make, with the result that adult children stop reporting them honestly. At public gatherings parents are just as prone as spouses to tell funny stories which demonstrate their superiority or remind the listeners that their grown offspring are still dependent upon them. The finest achievement of parenthood in the rest of the animal kingdom may be the attainment of full independence by the young of the species, but for homo sapiens the opposite seems very often to be true.

Confusion

In everyday relationships, it seems to me, there is often a fundamental confusion between dependence and love. To have somebody dependent on you, to be dependent on somebody else, these are interpreted as loving things to do. The confusion is enshrined in many of the ways loving and caring are expressed – 'I couldn't manage without you', 'You are the only thing I care about', 'Nobody else could possibly replace you.' Protecting and overprotecting extend dependence and are seen as ways of loving – 'Don't worry your pretty head about that!', 'Leave that to me, you know you're no good at it'. These are only a few of the thousands of ways dependence is increased and the power of the person being depended on is extended. Perhaps the most fascinating is the ploy which is expressed as 'I'm only doing it to help you', or 'It's for your own good.' The dependent person is forced to do something he or she doesn't want to do, or be seen as rejecting love.

Colonies

From time to time, of course, the system breaks down. People see through the confusion, or reject one partner in favour of another who can be better depended upon. But when it works well the system of 'loving' dependence enables really skilled operators to set themselves up as the strong protector and caring exploiter of a whole network of dependent relationships. There are many husbands, for example, whose wives and children are governed as colonies are governed by the Mother Country or the Fatherland. They are accorded privileges disguised as rights. If they are allowed to be self-governing at all, the 'colonial power' retains the right to suspend this arrangement on the grounds that it is being 'abused', meaning that it is against his own interests. Even after divorce – the equivalent of a grant of independence – there is often a long period of 'neo-colonialism', in which the former colony is economically or psycho-economically dependent on the former master.

No gain

It is this confusion between loving and dependence which causes the problem many grieving people fail to face. The 'colonial' system of relationships is valued, accepted, seldom questioned. Power and love form a powerful mixture. The dependent person has been taught, encouraged, manipulated, often over many years, into feeling inadequate without the person who had the power in the name of love. There has been no preparation for independence – no fostering beforehand of a stable, experienced government, no development of a self-sufficient, confident economy.

Maybe you have never thought about it this way before. Maybe all this does not apply to you, either as a former 'colony' or a former 'colonial power' that has lost its colony. Maybe you think it is all rather harsh, or cynical, or just too theoretical. But I urge you to think about it now.

If you have never been used to independence, the danger you face is that you look for another rescuer – a replacement for the protector you have lost. This is often why people re-marry in haste, and why so many of them and their partners repent at leisure. Exchanging one dependent relationship for another does not work. It takes years to make the system work – years of getting to know that one person inside-out-and-backwards – and it takes the resilient patience of youth to stick at it because failure would be unthinkable or hurt the children. The second time around is voluntary – and nobody becomes somebody else's colony voluntarily without keeping a door open somewhere which they can use to escape when the going gets rough. To swap one tyranny, however pleasant, for another is no gain.

Be patient

The answer is to try to realise why you were dependent, and to get rid of dependence as far and as fast as you can – to stand on your own feet, however shaky. You can be independent. You can learn to have your own self-confidence, your own friends, to value yourself and to trust your own feelings. There are others whose love and admiration you can accept because you and they are equals. You do not have to be beholden to a protecting power in order to qualify for a place in the world.

You will learn slowly, by making mistakes. But remember that you are used to having an impatient, critical voice telling you that you are not quite up to it all, that you should let somebody else do that. It is time to resist dependence, and to resist that impatient voice in your head. Love yourself more than you have been used to. Be patient with yourself. And learn.

9

Getting Used to Grief

As you get on with the work of grieving you get better at it. Of course things will never be the same as they used to be. But you begin to establish some control over the way they are different. You begin to realise that some aspects of what you have lost are things you didn't want anyway, but at the same time you had no choice but to accept them. You also start to see that some of the things you regretted before can be viewed in a different light. Old sores can heal if the irritants that caused them are allowed to fade into the past. Bereavement may take control of your life away from you, but grieving starts to bring it back again.

All this, of course, depends on how much of the work of grieving you do. It will only happen if you make progress in accepting the full reality of what you have lost, so that you avoid living in a world of make believe. It will not happen if you allow yourself to be isolated from contact and communication with people who matter and who do not have fixed ideas about how you ought to be – even if this means making new friends or asking strangers for help. Nor will you gain more control if you hand it over to another rescuer who, in any case, can only be a poor substitute for the one you may have lost.

Getting used to grief depends on making progress with the tasks of grieving. What signposts can you look out for to show you that you are on the road you want to take?

The badge of grief

Right at the beginning of your grieving, the most important fact in your life is that you have lost somebody. You are probably surrounded by people who are only there because of this fact. People call to see you, telephone you, write letters to you, who would not be in touch if your bereavement had not happened. And you have to go and see people to explain what has taken place or to make new arrangements because of it – officials whose help you need in order to register the change in your circumstances, or people you want to thank personally

71

for their kindness,

During this period, you are meeting people because of the bereavement, and so the most important fact they know about you is that you are grieving. They see this as part of your identity. Many of them will have been told, others you will have to tell yourself. And people will recognise you because of your loss – as the person who has just lost a husband or a wife, a parent or a child. Your loss, sometimes your grief, becomes a badge that people know you by.

Gradually the badge begins to fade. At first maybe you notice this happening by the way you are able to tell people without having to control your tears, or go into detail about what happened. Some people find that anger they felt when the bereavement happened, such as a need to seek out and find the person responsible for an ambulance arriving late, or to campaign in some way to have changes made so that the death will not have been so much in vain – this kind of anger begins to wear off a little. You do not feel any the less deeply the sense of your loss, but it becomes less important that other people recognise you only because of your loss.

These are all small pointers to the progress you are making in accepting your loss. They show that you now feel able to let other people accept you because of who you are rather than what has occurred. And the loss has become much more a part of who you are. Nevertheless, none of this happens without courage in tackling the pain and anguish of realisation – the doubting and questioning, the insecurity, crying and searching, the reassessment of your own special value as a person. These small signs of progress are hard won. You are entitled to wear them with a sense of inner pride as you give up the badge of grief.

For many people, the big landmark of this part of their development is making a new friend – one who was not a part of the first period of grief, who knew nothing of what happened. The value of this friendship is that you have won it for yourself as you now are – a person in your own right who does not need to be seen as bereaved in order to be recognised. Your new friend never knew the person you have lost. When, in friendship, you eventually talk about your grief, his or her reaction will be based on the reality of what you are and have achieved since, not on real knowledge of what you were like before. It will give you a chance to put down firm roots in a future which – only months before – you doubted you would ever live to see.

Feeling confident again

At the very least bereavement is an unsettling experience. Fundamentally it can shake your belief in yourself, in the safety of the world around you, in the certainty of life. It may be the first time you have ever experienced a death. From never thinking about life, you may have felt the ground cut off beneath your feet by the knowledge of how close death is to each of us. This experience can destroy your old, unquestioned peace, so that you can no longer sleep as you did, feel safe in the street the way you used to, or be secure in your own home.

As you begin to work at your grieving, small signs of progress appear in the re-emergence of your former confidence. One of the earliest is when you no longer accept passively that people feel you should not be left alone. At first you would not have questioned this. Then you find it slightly irritating. Further on, you are puzzled until you understand, and feel amused. Another early sign for many people is the return of their earlier sleep pattern, although there are also many people for whom this does not happen for a very long time – if at all, and who naturally establish a new and different routine.

But the main milestones are signs of confidence in your own decisions. You make up your mind more easily, and you worry less about whether you have done the right thing. This often starts with trivial decisions – what to eat, what to wear, where to go, what order you should do things in. As you begin to trust yourself, you start to trust other people more. You laugh more often. You stop having to ask people to repeat what they said because you did not hear or did not fully understand the first time. If you are living alone now, stray noises startle you less and you stop checking every single one. You can lock up once, instead of having to double- or treble-check the doors and windows.

More of what you do is because you want to do it, and more of it is done your way. At first, you merely continued the way things used to be. That way took account of the person you are

73

now missing. The new way does not. Some of the customs and rituals you both followed together get altered to make them easier. At first this feels wrong. But you get used to the changes and stop justifying them every time you use them. Bed-time rituals are the hardest to change for many people. When yours alter, this is usually a sign that you are accepting the realities and resisting dependence on the person for whom they were originally designed.

ritual
alter

Reminders

If you have lived with somebody a long time, and you lose that person, there will be plenty of things about to remind you of him or her. In the earliest days of grieving the natural reaction is to keep everything. This is part of the struggle to accept that he or she will never return to use those things again. As you go through the process of realisation, perhaps failing at first, the objects that belonged to him or her begin to change in value. Some of them will always be precious. Some are of no use now to you, but might be valued by another person. Yet others are not worth keeping. Half-consciously at first, then more deliberately and with greater confidence, you begin to design around you the nature of the memorial of small objects that you want to live with.

For many people there is a significant first time – the first time after a bereavement that they bought for themselves something they would usually have consulted about with the person who they have lost. Often it is relatively unimportant – nothing an outsider would recognise as very important. New furniture is often one such item, a new mirror, new crockery, or new clothes. The significance lies partly in not having consulted, and in the feeling that you like what you have chosen and it doesn't matter what he or she would have thought or said. But partly it is also another bit of acceptance. He or she would not know the house now, or recognise you in those clothes. Knowing this, and accepting it, means accepting also that he or she will not be coming back, will not be dismayed by what you have done, will not be reacting at all.

Now also you will find yourself wondering whether to go to places you went to together, or places you would have talked about to the person who is no longer there. Realisation is won very slowly at first. Maybe you are asked out by friends, feel reluctant to go, and fail to identify that this is because of past associations. Maybe you manage to see why you do not want to go, but cannot face the feeling of anxiety or of anger that arises – anxiety that it may be too painful to face those memories, anger that they should not have asked you, that they should have known. And if you can live without such feelings as these, will you feel that you can fit in when you get there? That you will be there in your own right? Unless you can do this, then the special memories will be too strong and defeat the purpose of going. You will not be able to enjoy yourself.

Maybe these feelings will not defeat you, and on that day you will pass another landmark, another piece of evidence that you are doing the work of grieving, and doing it well. Getting home afterwards could, however, be an even severer test. The greater landmark is passed when you go out somewhere you would have talked about, enjoy yourself, forget your missing partner, and come home to an empty house without feeling that the end of the adventure robbed the rest of all its savour.

Being an expert

Whoever you have lost, under whatever circumstances, if you are grieving it is because you were special to one another in some way. Part of your task is to accept that you will never be special to somebody in exactly the same way ever again. In the deepest crisis of grief, this reality may seem unacceptable, so that your life seems to be meaningless. When you have committed yourself to life, its meaning will return. You begin to 'de-specialise' – to dismantle parts of your life and behaviour which only made sense to that person or because of that person, and to replace them with new parts that make sense generally.

People often underestimate just how far they had become 'specialised'. But just think for a moment about how much you knew about the person you have lost. You have a great deal of specialised knowledge – not just about the things he or she did, but also about his or her personality. You may have been the only one who really knew that person well, as well, in

75

fact, as any one person can know another person. You knew a great deal about how to communicate with the person – and probably how not to! If you live with somebody for a long time, you forget how much effort went into learning to get along together, and yet it all produces highly specialised skills and knowledge on your part. Somebody once told me that when she looked back on thirty years of marriage, she had in fact spent most of her life 'getting to know one man extremely well'.

When an academic specialises in one subject and gets to know it very deeply, other people often regard him as rather out of touch with general matters. He is seen as only functioning really well when he is dealing with his 'own' subject. There is usually a lot of truth in this. Something similar may have happened to you. You are used to your special knowledge and skills, and used to using them with that special person. The academic expert never has the time to study general matters. In the same way, there have probably been restrictions on your time and opportunity to get to know a wide range of other people.

So when the person you 'specialised' in is no longer there, what happens? First, of course, you know a great deal that you will never be able to use again, except when you talk about that person. This used to be important every time you were together, but now, although it is still important, the value of it is bound to fall. Other people will not want you to spend the whole of your time for the rest of your life talking to them about that person. They will want to hear about you and what you have been doing recently – not about the past, however interesting.

For some people, therefore, the first time they hear another person talk about their specialised subject – the person they have lost – without even feeling the need to add information, take over the conversation, or correct wrong impressions or facts, is a major step forward. Maybe all they have realised is that they 'have to stop going on about it' the way they did at first, or that 'other people need to have their say', but even this cannot be done without the courage to face and to accept painful feelings. You have made real progress if you have learned that part of your own value needs to change as a result of loss.

76

Communication skills

The second consequence of no longer having with you the person in whom you have become specialised, is that some of the ways you deal with other people may have been right for him or her – but they are not right for them. They may be almost right, but not quite right. This is particularly likely to happen with some of the more 'special' of your specialised skills, those which two people develop to deal with their strongest feelings – being angry with one another, being afraid of one another, and feeling sexual towards one another.

The art of being angry with somebody whom you are very close to is always a specialised subject. So much depends on how well you know that person, so you can read the tiny nuances of each reaction, and on how well that person knows you and what you are likely to be thinking at every stage of a disagreement. When somebody feels hurt or angry his actions are often designed to make the other person feel exactly as bad as he does – not just a little bit more, or a little bit less, but exactly. This takes great skill, and can only be learned by getting to know the other person. Anything less than the exact amount will mean the other person has not understood fully, and if you hurt the other person more than you feel hurt, then it may be too late to say 'Sorry, I didn't mean what I said.' Knowing exactly what hurts somebody takes a long time.

It is just as difficult to learn how to deal with fear. When you are close to somebody, there may still be times when the things he or she does make you feel frightened – either scared of the person or afraid for him or her. When two people know one another very well they also know how much of this anxiety to reveal to one another, and how much to hide. But at first they do not. This is how hidden feelings in a relationship arise in the first place, and one of the ways dependence is extended by the dominant partner. It leads to a highly specialised set of communication skills, but very few of those who have them realise just how specialised the skills are.

It is not difficult to see that something very similar is likely to happen to sexual feelings also. If you find somebody sexually attractive, particularly in a normal relationship where there is dependence by one person on the other for, say, financial or emotional security, comfort, protection, love and affection, then how can you express exactly what you feel? Maybe you feel only mildly interested in sex – more a need for a cuddle than for anything more athletic. If you get the signals wrong you will mislead the other person into thinking you want either more than this or less than this. Wrong sexual signals in a dependent relationship may provoke anger or fear, and as a result you get less of the things you depend on that person for – less security, less comfort, less love and affection. So in normal relationships many people learn the highly specialised skills of knowing just how much of their sexual arousal to show or to hide – skills which would not apply to anybody else in the world. Also, their sexual experience tends to be limited to relationships where there is dependence.

Setting up any new relationship which is important enough for you to need to be able to deal with anger and fear and sexual feelings together as a couple can be an exciting adventure. To succeed means learning a whole set of new specialised behaviour, tailor-made to you and that person and to nobody else in precisely the same way. What will always result in failure is you or the other person treating one another as somebody else. The failure may not be a disaster, but unless you realise how specialised you have become, you may never learn how to become really important to the people you meet who matter most to you.

Progress

At the start of grief, of course, the idea of ever again becoming really special to somebody else may be the last thing you want to consider. But if you do the work of grieving, and realise that for you, being special is a necessary part of any real commitment to life, then this will be a big step forward. You will find yourself reacting to people in anger or anxiety. Recognising the tendency we all have to use older, specialised ways of reacting – to snap back without thinking, to bottle up important feelings – all the habits formed in earlier, longer relationships, will be a real test of your progress. Openly admitting what you have done, and committing yourself to learning new ways will show you can resist dependence on the person you like, and resist the isolation that comes from giving up the struggle to be important to somebody else.

Even if you want to be important to people, you may not not want to be sexually important. This is right for some people, and not right for others. But sadly, many of those who do not want a sexual relationship ever again fail to realise how much of their old, specialised communication was to do with things like being attractive and pleasant, with touching to show pleasure, with accepting or rejecting the right others have to be sexual. So they stop being attractive in case it might be taken as wanting sex. They reject even friendly touching, and show disgust when they see men and women and children who display delight in being sexual. Unfortunately, too, the people they reject in this way are often their own children and grandchildren. Learning to believe compliments, to be attractive again in a general way, to accept sexuality begins in your own family. But not without courage even here.

10

Setbacks and Reaffirmation

You still have work to do. At times now the event which started your grieving seems a long way behind you. There are other times when it seems that it happened only yesterday or earlier today. Your whole personality, through the conscious and unconscious effort you have put into tackling the tasks of grief, has begun to free itself from the trauma and grow again. The signs show that you may be over the worst. Many, many people reach this stage a year and a half, two years after a serious loss. Others take longer, in excess of three years. The time cannot be predicted. The time does not really matter, either, for recovery and growth do not go by the clock but depend on how much damage was done and how resilient the organism was before the damage.

The same pattern of realisation that occurred during the early moments of grief is still there. Now it takes longer to work through it, because you are dealing with larger matters than your mind could handle before. You become at times a little less sensitive to your own feelings, particularly if you were not used to being very sensitive before the trauma. So you need to use the process of realisation more consciously, sit down and think about it more, to talk things over more deeply with those who are affected by your lack of realisation. You still need to question your reactions, to face up to doubts and explore the reasons for them. You still need to feel your insecurity, to connect anger and fear not to their apparent immediate causes, but to the elements of your loss which your mind has still been unable to accept. You will also feel alienated at times from other people, and fail to break out of this – usually because you underestimate your own specialness or cannot fully appreciate that other people are special also.

This is not the end of grieving, but it marks the transition from having a life dominated by grief to having a grief dominated by life. When you get this far you will face a period of setbacks rather than failures, of reaffirmations, rededications rather then crises. It will be time to look back and see what is behind you, whilst also recognising that there is still work you must do now that you are living with grief.

An overview

You can now look back at what happened and see something like a whole picture. What is there still left to do in the major task of accepting the full reality of what you have lost? Is there something important you have still been unable to face, or are there only small bits and pieces to fit into the jigsaw?

These are questions you can only answer in detail for yourself. But if there is some major issue you have not faced up to it will almost certainly be because it was there before your bereavement, and you could not face up to it then either. If you are going to be able to tackle it now, then this will be for two reasons – first, because you already know deep within yourself what it is, even if you have never discussed it with anybody, and secondly, because it is something about yourself which you could not change while the person you have lost was alive, but which has become easier to change because he or she is now dead.

A brief example will help to show the kind of thing I mean. Joyce, whom I mentioned earlier to help illustrate the pattern of realisation, heard the news of her husband's death from her friend Helen, who became her main support over the next eighteen months. Joyce found out more about the circumstances. Graham had died in the ambulance with Helen holding him in her arms. His attack had taken place while Graham had been upstairs and naked in Helen's bed. There had been no time to pick up his clothes when the ambulance came, and the hospital had assumed that Helen was Graham's wife. Helen had not challenged this assumption. One possible interpretation, of course, is that Graham and Helen were having an affair, and that the heart attack may even have happened whilst they were making love.

I first met Joyce about three months after her bereavement, and was her counsellor for about half a dozen sessions spread over two months. She knew all this by then, and the possibility that there had been an affair was obvious to me. I made no attempt to confront her with the idea since when I went over the facts in a non-interpretive way she drew absolutely no conclusions for herself. She was simply not puzzled, and clearly did not have on her agenda any doubts about Graham's fidelity that she wanted to work through with me.

When these sessions ended I heard nothing from her until two years after Graham's death. Then she made an appointment saying she 'thought she would be over it all by now, but wasn't'. We had two more sessions, the first very tentative while she went over the facts several times, not really knowing why she felt the need to. At the start of the second session I confronted her with the possibility that there had been an affair.

Yes, she admitted, there was a real possibility, and she had thought about it. But Helen had been very kind and loving, and because of this Joyce had pushed the thought to the back of her mind. Now she began to explore her feelings, opening them up for the first time. By the end she had accepted that if there had been an affair it had taken nothing away from her marriage or the love she had had for Graham. She had, she said, known she felt this way long before her bereavement but had suppressed the feeling. She had wanted him to be happy, to die as a happy person, and the fact that he had been with somebody he loved and who loved him was good – however that love might have been expressed. She said she could accept an affair, and not being told about it by Helen, without feeling threatened or angry. But it was obvious as she spoke that she was not yet ready to think about the idea of Graham and Helen in bed together on that fateful day. As she left she told me, 'I need to work on that by myself still. That's why I'm not over it yet.'

Joyce had already known – without fully realising – what had been troubling her and delaying the completion of her grief. The problem went back a long way before her bereavement and had been one of the problems of her marriage. She had loved Graham, wanted him to be happy, but had long been afraid of him having affairs, even if this meant he would be happy. Unable to face this fear completely she had found a compromise for herself. She decided that she would not ask if he had affairs, and hoped he would not tell her if he found somebody else. All she wanted, if he was happier elsewhere, was that he would not leave her. By not-asking, and encouraging him to not-tell her, she was able to contain her fear and her anger whenever she suspected infidelity. Over the last year or so Graham had seemed happy, and she had not-asked herself why in case she could not live with the answer.

This kind of response to suspected infidelity is very common in marriages, and perhaps if Helen had acted differently, Joyce would have faced her fear and anger early on in her grief. But Helen was loving and kind, and very supportive even though she was grieving herself. Joyce had come to depend on her, in much the same way as she had depended on Graham. Because Joyce did not want to lose Helen's support or to hurt Helen, she applied the same compromise and encouraged Helen to not-tell her, at the same time not-asking.

When I phoned her a few weeks after our last session she had resolved the problem. She had decided positively, not out of fear or anger, that it would be best if she never knew. The decision had been 'a great relief,' and she felt very much better. 'I'm going to let it rest there,' she said.

Being vaguely uneasy

The kind of setbacks you have during this period of transition will help you to see whether you still have a lot of work to do in your grieving, or only a little. As we saw from Joyce's story, you may think you are no longer grieving, and then become aware that you still feel vaguely unhappy with your progress. It is important when this happens to look back and see what you wanted to change in the lost relationship before the bereavement, and what you wanted to keep the same even though you knew in your heart that this was not possible. Next, see if you have some new options. Maybe you had no choice then, and now have choice. Maybe you are still spending a lot of your energy trying to resist change the way you used to when this was vitally necessary, even though it is now unnecessary. If you are doing this, and can find out why, then you can make a conscious decision about it – instead of unconsciously saving up energy for something that will never happen again.

In this way little questions can be unanswered – we do not always need to know the whole truth. Big ones can be looked at afresh to see whether they are still worth all the trouble they used to cause you. If they are worth the energy you are spending on them, then it is best to spend that energy by trying to change for positive reasons, rather than spending it on bottling up feelings that are negative and destructive.

83

More about change

Big setbacks, then, mean that you have to change yourself –
your attitudes, your sensitivity, your ability to live with
uncomfortable truths. Change has to be 'realised'. It cannot
be left to chance, and this means you will need to tackle it
consciously and with courage. It will help you to apply what
has already been said about the process of realisation directly
to yourself in a systematic and methodical way.

Remember that the first stage is defining what you want to
change. But this is not much use if all you come up with is a
vague area of doubt. Change has to be specific, or it cannot be
realised. If you cannot be specific, however, then this also tells
you something. Either you need to try harder, or you are not
yet ready to change and need to accept your unreadiness.
There will be other chances if you really want them. An
inability to be specific might also be because it isn't you who
wants to change, but somebody else who wants you to alter.
Maybe you are not resisting pressure effectively enough. So
you need to ask whether you want change for yourself or for
somebody else. Changing to please somebody else is dangerous – it will increase dependency, isolate you from your true
feelings, and seldom works however hard you try. What's
more you know all this anyway. So you need to define the
specific change you want to make. Often this is enough,
because when people do this they have to face their doubts
about themselves, and these turn out to be worth keeping.
Somebody who thinks maybe she should work harder, for
example, because she is lazy, may discover that she isn't lazy
once she really questions herself. The doubt is not worth
keeping because it doesn't fit the evidence. Or suppose somebody wants to be more attractive. When he tries to be specific
about what he wants to change, and faces his doubts, there is a
good chance that all he wants is reassurance that he really is
attractive already.

Securing change

To accomplish a specific change, you need to move to the
second level of realisation – the one to do with feeling the
need to be secure. The best way to test your feelings at this

stage is to set yourself a specific time-frame. Ask yourself when you are going to make the change – when you will start, and when it will have been made. Are you going to act now? Tomorrow? What time tomorrow? If you are not able to fix a time to start and a time when you will have accomplished the change, and just come up with vague answers like 'sometime soon' or 'when I get round to it', then the chances are that you are scared of the change or angry about having to make it. Both these reasons are enough justification not to commit yourself. But they also mean you have not been specific enough at the definition stage. Go back and reconsider whether change is really necessary.

If the change you need to make is clear, however, and you have a specific time-frame in mind, the next step is to ask yourself whether the change you want to make is within your own gift. That is to say, are you in charge of all the things which you want to alter? The change must be one which depends only on your own actions. You cannot be certain of accomplishing it if it depends on other people. Too much might go wrong. Asking this question also helps a lot of people to see that the real problem is not being tackled. If what they really want is for other people to change while they remain virtually the same, then this can indicate one of two things – either they are dependent on others and have not reduced their dependence, or they are isolated from others and cannot communicate their anger or fear at the way they are being treated.

Proof

Suppose you get this far – the change you want to make is specific, you can secure it in a finite period of time, and you own the means to achieve it yourself. Now you reach the fourth stage. Again you need to be clear and methodical about your intentions. When you have made the change, how will you know precisely that it has worked? What proof will there be? If 'people' will treat you better, for example, who specifically are these people? What are their names? And how will you know? If you will 'feel better', how precisely will you feel better? What differences will be noticeable?

Asking yourself these questions – or talking them over in

this way with a good helper – can enable you to achieve real changes instead of making vague resolutions that do not get carried out. If any of the work of grieving has not been done fully, then you will not be able to apply this process through to its conclusion in real change which can be proven to have been accomplished. You will need to accept some part of your reality that you have been avoiding, or re-think your commitment to a full life. You may need help also – the process is a lot easier when you let somebody guide you through it. And the work of resisting isolation, and dependence will have to go on too. If you cannot make the changes in your self or in your circumstances that you most want to make, then you are probably trying too hard to be what other people want you to be, and have not done enough yet to sort out what you want for yourself.

11

Helping People Grieve

One of the main tasks facing the grieving person is to be realistic about asking for and accepting help. This is by no means an easy task, for a wide range of reasons. For example, there may be nobody immediately available due to the geographical isolation of the bereaved, or those people who are available may not be capable of help, or trusted to help. At the same time, the need for assistance can be desperate. Bereavement can leave dependants materially impoverished, threatened with homelessness and hunger. It can leave them psychologically devastated, shocked, hurt, bewildered, and with nowhere to turn. They may need to tackle the immediate problems of bereavement with help from other people – indeed, this is almost always the case – before there is much likelihood of them tackling the tasks of grieving.

So far we have looked at grief mainly from the point of view of the person who has suffered the loss. But we also need to look at it from the point of view of the person being asked for help. From the start, bereavement, and then grief, place considerable strain not only on the resources of those closest to the person who has died, but also on those whose assistance is needed. You may be asked to help as a member of the same family, as a friend, as a concerned neighbour, or as a new aquaintance. Or you may not be asked to help, but want to be asked, and not know how best to deal with this situation. What kind of help can you give? And how can you be sure that you are giving the right kind of help?

Some answers will already have emerged by implication – obviously the first step is to understand grief in general, and to know what the tasks are that face the grieving person. Your help might be required at the beginning with day-to-day practical matters which the bereaved cannot handle due to an immediate lack of resources – lack of health or strength, skill, time, money, or friends and family. Or it might be needed to help them through the very first stages of grief – breaking the news, being there when they emerge from shock, helping them through the life-death crisis as their grieving progresses. You may also find yourself helping with late setbacks, or

87

delayed grieving. At the same time you will very often have your own grieving to do. The kind of help you can give, and whether or not you are doing the right thing, are issues which depend in detail on your own circumstances and those of the bereaved person.

We are simply not going to be able to deal with all these issues in great detail here. But what we can do is look at the main principles of helping so you can apply them to your own case. We also consider the kind of communication skills you will need, and look at the problems which seem to cause most difficulty to helpers in general. Particularly specialised problems – those which arise from added difficulty due to the way somebody died – are examined in several of the later chapters.

Practical help

The most important point about help is that it has to be practical. You are not helping if you cost the person energy, make a task harder to complete in the time available, or 'crowd' the other person so that he or she is not given the necessary 'space'. For example, costing somebody energy can happen if you make yourself a nuisance by insisting they need your help when they say they do not. It can happen if you pretend to be helping with their grief only to get more attention from them in dealing with your own feelings. You can cost somebody energy by helping and then making it plain that you also need to be rewarded with gratitude.

Also, you can make life harder for somebody by turning a simple task which should not take long into a complicated one which takes far longer. Time pressure is increased when we dramatise or exaggerate the need to act immediately – telling a person he or she must get over the misery at once, for example, or move house straight away, or drop everything else and put a particular task at the top of the list. As for pressure on space – we increase this for a person whenever we 'crowd' him or her, that is to say, whenever we interfere on the grounds that we know a better way of doing something, or refuse to leave them alone to get on with work they are trying to do. Offering to help, and then taking up basic resources of energy, time, and space, destroys any practical advantage which our assistance might otherwise have provided.

So whenever you act as a helper you have to be sure you are not increasing the other person's dependence on you for more than extremely short periods of time, if at all. How can you be sure of this?

As a free gift

The only way that really works is to give free gifts of your own energy, time and space. A free gift is something you enable a person to control totally, without reservation or qualification, and without counting the cost to yourself, or estimating any profit that may come to you as a result. If you give freely neither you nor the person you are giving to becomes less independent in any way. Now, of course, there are problems with this idea, and you have to be aware of them and find a way of solving them. The first problem is that you cannot give what you do not have to spare. Otherwise you will resent giving, be forced to count the cost, and ultimately be no use to yourself, let alone the person you wanted to help. Giving out of a sense of duty often leads to this. For example, adult children often feel it is their duty to do more than they can realistically manage for a bereaved parent. Insisting that Mum or Dad comes to live with you whatever the difficulties sounds fine and loving, but often it is the whole family that suffers and Mum or Dad ends up being tolerated rather than loved. To take another example, sparing time to pop in and see a bereaved neighbour when you are already in a great hurry to go somewhere else, and cannot really spare the time, will make matters worse for both of you, not help your neighbour who may need far more time than you have available. It is better to go later, and have time to give freely, rather than to 'make time' for people and either resent this, or cause problems for yourself and those who were waiting elsewhere for you by turning up late and using the grieving person as an excuse.

Whatever help you give can only be a free gift if you can spare it and carry the cost of it yourself. Using it on somebody else should not hurt or threaten a third party. Nor should it limit your capacity to go on helping. Clearly it would be nonsense to give away everything you have – your whole time, energy, space, property, and so on – if this makes you even more in need of help than the person you have given it all to, or if people who depend on you will have nothing either. Whatever you give, whatever the cost, it must be your cost, not somebody else's and you have to preserve your capacity to go on being useful to the people around you.

Demanding

The danger of giving energy, time, and space that you cannot afford calls for some fine judgement on your part. And that leads us to the second problem – that this need to make judgements about what you can spare can easily be confused with 'counting the cost'. How can it be true on the one hand that the best way to help is to give without counting the cost, if you also have to calculate in advance what you can spare. Besides, isn't it rather mean only to give what you can spare? Wouldn't it be more generous and loving to give more than this and not to calculate at all?

Two quite different things are being mixed up here. First there is the question of cost. Strictly speaking giving without counting the cost means giving without making somebody else pay any part of the cost. You expect nothing back in return, and you help the other person on no other basis than this. But there is also the question of 'price' – something quite different from 'cost'.

The price of an object or service is what you have to pay out of your own resources in order to obtain it. This is not the same as either the value of the object, or what it will cost you to have the object. For example, if you buy a car for a low price, its value might be higher than what you pay. But it may cost you far more than the price you paid to own the car and to use it. Let us apply this idea to the problem of helping a person who is grieving.

What you need to calculate carefully is the price of helping. You need to be sure what energy, time, and space you will have to give up in order to be in a position to help. You have to do this in advance. Once you have started helping it will be too late – you will have committed yourself. It is no use blaming the other person if he or she does not value your help and does not take your advice, and does not feel grateful. If these are what you thought you were buying, and none of them appears, that is your risk as the purchaser – and not the fault of the person you are helping. Being angry because your investment did not pay off is your problem – not the problem of the person you wanted to help.

So before you spend your own resources on helping somebody, be sure you know what your own expectations and motives are, and that you know the risks and are prepared to pay the price. Above all, make sure that he or she wants you to have an opportunity to give real help. It is no good forcing somebody to accept help. Take 'no' for an answer. If you work hard at insisting that somebody you want to help must accept your help, then what are you doing? You are raising the price you have to pay, whilst at the same time he or she is telling you that the value of your help at present is low. And the more you insist on raising the price you want to pay, the more suspicious he or she gets, and the value of your offered help goes down and down.

Being a nuisance

People who want to help, but who do not calculate the price of their opportunity to help in advance, who do not think through what it is they are trying to obtain by helping, and who do not make sure their help is really wanted, are a menace. They always end up making their victims pay, and being a thorough nuisance. Fortunately there are ways of recognising them by the things they say while they are 'helping'.

One typical call of this predatory bird is, 'It's for your own good!' This is an attempt to disguise the fact that they are really helping for their own good. They have paid the price, thinking they were buying control over the person they said they wanted to help, and this is their way of trying to exercise power. They feel they have a right to be heard and obeyed because of the energy and time they have spent. Another similar call is 'I'm only trying to help you.' This means they are only trying to help themselves to what they think they have paid for. 'You don't have to feel grateful' is another piece of deception – it means the direct opposite.

This species of nuisance is usually territorial, too. Having paid for their chance to control somebody, the last thing they will do is allow somebody else to muscle in on the piece of property they have purchased. They get very jealous if help is accepted from elsewhere. Other helpers 'don't know what they are talking about' or are 'not worth listening to'. If a rival helper hoves into view, their necks bristle, and they try to drive the intruder away – perhaps by saying that he or she is not one of the family or has no right to interfere. I remember one good example of this – the organiser of a 'helping' group in a hospital, who refused absolutely to let qualified counsellors near the group because it was 'only for the staff of this hospital' and she knew there were no counsellors on the staff.

Another sign that the helper thinks he or she has paid for an element of control is the look of hurt innocence that appears when advice is refused or ignored, particularly the kind of advice which begins, 'If you take my advice' or 'If I were you'. Some people are so used to managing others that they feel this is their greatest skill, and are hurt when people want to manage themselves. They want you to like them, and to enjoy being controlled by them. If you show you don't want this, they put on a hurt look so you will feel sorry for them and continue to let them be clever by letting them control you – at your cost.

Being there

Making somebody else pay the costs of your help, or using the offer of help to further your own conscious and unconscious needs for power and attention – these deprive the grieving person of resources he or she desperately needs. But if you can make a free gift of energy, time, and space that you know will not run out for the foreseeable future, then you can help a great deal. Giving energy usually means doing tasks for people, such as little things like shopping or cooking, or helping with correspondence. It can also mean having the energy to let them share their bewilderment and frustration without becoming either bewildered or frustrated yourself. Giving a free gift of time and space probably helps the most – just being there, not doing anything to them or for them, or managing their problems for them. Being with somebody is very difficult for some people – they are not used to being valuable without actually doing anything. All their lives they have only been rewarded for doing or having, and never for just being. This may be true of you. When all you are asked for is your presence, this is the truest of compliments. If it makes you feel impatient, then try to relax and to feel the same thing the person you are being with is feeling.

There is no need to make conversation, or to fill in the pauses with activity. You are needed for the most basic reason of all, that you are a qualified member of the human race. That is enough. Stay in touch by looking. If you can, pace your breathing to match that of the other person, and it oftens helps also if you sit in a similar position. If physical contact is acceptable, then hold the other person's hand or put an arm round his or her shoulders as you would a child. It doesn't matter what sex either of you is if you touch the right way – in a relaxed and gentle manner, not trapping the other person, ready to remove your hand or arm effortlessly if he or she seems to want you to stop touching, and making sure that your touch is not a caress that might, under other circumstances, be sexually arousing for either of you.

If the other person cries, do not do anything except accept this. Trying to cheer him or her up means you will stop just being there, and start becoming the manager of that person's feelings. There is nothing more frustrating or annoying than having somebody try to dry your eyes and stop you crying when you need to weep. What is more it shows that the helper cannot or dare not allow you to have your own feelings. The helper turns into an angry, impatient parent, who doesn't care what you feel, as long as he or she does not feel uncomfortable. I remember having my face slapped, and actually being punched by such a 'helper' quite recently when I needed to grieve and to share my crying with somebody. He had been taught that grown men do not cry.

Being a good listener

Being with somebody without doing anything to take over is part and parcel of being a good listener. It is the basis of what are called 'counselling skills'. Counselling is a widely abused and misunderstood term. It does not mean 'listening sympathetically and giving advice' as many people think it does. Counselling means listening with empathy – being part of the other person, not a critical outsider, however well-meaning or

93

JOHN RYLANDS UNIVERSITY LIBRARY

gentle. It means seeing the world from the other person's point of view, and not making moral judgements or being shocked by the way that person perceives things.

Even if you have had no training in counselling skills, you can do a great deal to help people by learning some of them yourself. If you are helping somebody, remember that he or she is the most important person present. Don't take over and start managing. Let that person do the talking, and just nod or murmur and smile to show you are listening, at the same time staying in touch by looking at his or her eyes even if this is not returned all the time. There is no danger of 'staring' and putting them off if you look in a relaxed, warm and friendly way – rather like the touch described earlier. If you need to ask questions this should only be to help the person explore feelings for himself or herself, and not because you want to confirm some idea of your own about why something happened so you can see if one of your solutions will work.

You will help most if you use only 'open' questions – the sort that leaves it open to the other person to answer whichever way suits him or her. Questions which end with phrases like 'isn't it' or 'aren't you' demand the answer 'no'. Questions which use the words 'do you think', 'don't you think', 'do you feel', 'don't you see' and so on, are disguised imperatives. In effect they are telling the person what to think, feel, or see. They are all right for everyday relationships, perhaps, but not for helping somebody to have feelings and feel free to express or explore them.

One of the best kinds of questions you can use is what I call the 'one-word' question. What you do is to listen intently and choose a word the other person used which seems to be significant – either because it understates or overstates a feeling that you know the other person has. A good listener can hear such key-words in almost every phrase if the speaker feels safe enough to talk openly and honestly. You keep yourself aware of each new example, so you always have at least three or four recent ones in your consciousness. Then, when the speaker pauses, you wait. If he or she continues after a long pause, you carry on giving extra attention to the key-words. But if the pause shows that the speaker does not know what to say, you choose the most recent key-word and turn it into a one-word question. This is done simply by repeating the word with a question in your voice, and then waiting. It is an invitation from you to the person to explore this feeling further.

Jump leads

Good counselling is rather like helping a neighbour whose car has a flat battery. Your own car battery has to be well-charged or you cannot help. Indeed, you will reduce your chances of being able to help if you put your car out of action as well as failing to start your neighbour's. In the same way, if you cannot deal with your own feelings, and try to help somebody else explore his or hers you will only become a burden to him or her. It will stir up anger or fear in you and he or she will not only find you no help, but may end up having to rescue you.

If you have a well-charged battery, the next step is to connect the two batteries together using the 'jump leads'. This is like establishing mutual contact in counselling. The energy will not flow unless it is a two-way process. If only one lead is connected, no energy flows, and if the connection is wrong, your own battery may be damaged or drained completely. Neither of you will benefit.

Once a mutual connection is established the neighbour is able to take what energy he needs to start his car. Obviously if there is not enough energy, you have to break off and suggest he uses another neighbour's help. In counselling and helping, it is very important to recognise your limitations. If you cannot help, say so, and be honest about it. Don't make the problem worse by going beyond your capabilities. Hopefully, however, the neighbour's car will start – in counselling the equivalent of this is that the person you are helping feels better able to do what he or she wants to do, whatever that happens to be.

But you have not finished yet. You now have to disconnect the jump leads. You do not drive off with the two batteries connected. Nor do you let the other person do this. And you do not get into the wrong car. The good helper is also careful to disconnect, and not to carry on his or her involvement by trying to live the other person's life for him, or tell him or her where to go next, or let the person being helped become dependent.

Helping to realise

The most welcome words you can ever hear when you are helping somebody with the tasks of grief are 'Now I realise'. This only happens when the person you are working with has connected up another part of the reality he or she could not previously accept. If you are already an experienced helper, and know how to use counselling skills, then you can set out to achieve this kind of response by studying and understanding the pattern of realisation described earlier.

The first step is to enable the person you are helping to concentrate on doubts and to feel safe whilst questioning whatever is important to him or her. For example, he or she might want to question the way certain uncomfortable feelings have arisen. What is uncomfortable about them? Have they occurred before? When was this? A person who did not cry at the loss of a loved one may, for instance, wonder why, or feel guilty about this. You help him explore what he feels, to question it, and to define his feelings. The next step will be to help him accept the insecurity this brings, the need to complain, to be angry or afraid, the need to cry, or to cry out about it. You do this by showing that his value, worth as a person, and lovability is unimpaired by having feelings of distress. No reassurance will be needed if you keep empathy, stay in touch as a warm, caring human presence, and show that he is not rejected for having feelings that he was afraid to have or angry about having. He will find self-assurance from the fact that you are not shocked or critical towards him.

This will get you through the first and second stages into the third stage of realisation. Here the person begins to face up to his need to search for a solution others will either accept or reject. He will want to speculate about their reaction. For example, if he has not wept, and people in his immediate circle are important to him, he will wonder aloud what they thought. He will also want to know for himself what they will do if he talks to them about his feelings. Any problem of relationships, including grief problems, has the effect, amongst others, of isolating people from those groups to which they belong. You have not rejected him, but he is afraid they might, or angry because they already have. Help him explore this as far as he wants to go. At the back of the fear or anger, there will

96

probably be a pattern of behaviour established during child-hood, so this stage can take a long time. Only if he is aware of having learned his response, and that he can learn a new one to replace it, can he move fully into the fourth stage.

Here the focus is on his need to be special, to accept his right to have his own special and unique feelings. He may need to look at the evidence of past problems to see that he has always had the courage to face reality before, or to see that he need not be afraid this time. When he accepts his specialness, he can usually complete the realisation.

Self-help

Being a good listener and just being there is practical help. It enables the grieving person to think aloud and 'feel aloud'. It helps him or her to come to terms with feelings and get them into proportion.

But you cannot help everyone. If you have a power rela-tionship with somebody – and many family relationships are also power relationships – then this sets limits on what you can do. If you experience any impatience when you are trying to help, stop as soon as you can, and leave the matter there. You will only be giving third-class help at best. Second-class help usually comes from the concerned stranger who has good counselling skills. This is because it enables the grieving person to find the best help of all, the first class help called self-help.

12

Grief Before Death

Grief sometimes starts before the death of the person who is loved. When you know that somebody who is close to you will die soon, and you begin to try to grasp this fact, you are already trying to accept the reality of that death even though it has not yet happened, and even though your whole being may want to reject the idea that it is now inevitable. What are the special demands made on us by grief for a loved one under these circumstances? What extra resources do we need if we are to live with such grief, and how are we to find them? These are some of the questions we shall look at next. Perhaps your own grief began this way, or is only just beginning. It can happen when you know that somebody near to you has lived a full life and is now gently nearing a peaceful end to that life. And it can happen because somebody dear to you is dying slowly and prematurely from an incurable illness.

When you are faced with such a grief, the tasks of grieving are the same – you still need to realise and to accept the full extent of what you are losing. You will still be confronted by the crisis of commitment, and have to resolve from the testing of your own courage whether you can go on and for how long. You will need to decide about help, and to set new limits on your willingness to seek it. The tasks of resistance cannot be ignored either. Like all grieving people you will need to resist becoming isolated. If you allow yourself to become cut off from people who care about you by the things you feel and the things you have to do, and withdraw out of anger or fear from your rightful place in the world, then you may never be able to reclaim that place as your own. And you will need to resist dependence. You alone must be in charge of what you do, what you think, what you feel. If you hand over responsibility for any of these things to somebody else, and let them treat you as their object, however precious, you will become less of a person in your own right. You need to be yourself, not the property of somebody you have to please. You need to be free to do, think, and feel what is right for you, so that when you make compromises you know exactly where you stand and what you are letting yourself in for.

When you begin to grieve for somebody who is still alive, the tasks before you are the same ones any bereaved person has to face. But the circumstances under which you start them, and the difficulties which you will encounter as you set about completing those tasks are different. Sometimes, knowing a person is going to die can make the work of grieving very much easier. Sometimes it makes it harder. To understand the special nature of the problem we need to begin by exploring the reasons why this is so.

A peaceful death

Knowing in advance that somebody is going to die can, under certain circumstances, help us to make the work of grieving into a beautiful and enriching experience. The sadness is still there. Courage is still required from those who grieve. But a very large part of the grief work of those concerned seems lighter because it is shared in a loving way between them. Grief becomes a preparation for bereavement. When the death occurs it is a deeply moving and very sad event, but it is not distressing, and there is a soft and peaceful transition into bereavement and loss.

This is what happened, for example, when a friend of mine whom I shall call Peter, lost his mother. A few weeks before she died, she visited each member of her family to say good-bye. She and they already knew that she had a terminal illness. She helped each one of them in turn to accept that she really was going to die. Peter told me that he and his mother had cried together. 'I don't want you to die,' he said. For a while she comforted him as if he were a baby again. Then she said, 'I don't want to die. But it has to be done.' As she wept with him this time it seemed that she was a frightened child whom he could comfort. 'Then we met as equals,' Peter told me. They discussed where she would die, and she told him that she loved him and would like him to be there if this was possible. 'But I may not have much say in what happens,' she said. 'And I may not recognise people. So I want to say my biggest good-bye now. I shall see all I can of everybody before then, but there will only be little good-byes after this.'

Peter was not able to be with her when she died, but he felt as though he had been, and the reality of her death has been easier to accept, he thinks, because of this. She helped him see that he could go on with his life glad she had been part of that life, and accepting that she would still be part of it after her death. He felt closer to life because of her. He felt no sense of isolation from her or from the rest of his family, and this was partly because she had said a special goodbye to each of them. In telling her that he did not want her to die, and in accepting that she did not want to leave him, Peter had also been enabled to end part of his babyhood, a part of it which had survived into his adult life as an unreal dependence upon her. He had given up a significant part of his need to be helpless and lost without her presence.

Clearly Peter himself was able to start work on the tasks of grief under these circumstances, and to go a very long way towards completing them. But what made this so much easier was his mother's behaviour. She needed to come to terms with what was happening to her also. The dying have their own need to grieve. We cannot claim truly to have understood grief until we have recognised and accepted this fact, and faced up to all its implications.

The grief of the dying

Maybe grief is not a reality to most people until they choose to make it so, or are forced by events to face their own feelings about dying. One way this can happen, as we have seen, is through bereavement. But it can also happen to people when they become aware of the imminence of their own death. Grief is essentially the way we react to significant loss, and somebody who knows that he or she will soon lose life itself needs to grieve for the loss of that life. Of course, the circumstances may prevent this from happening, as when death strikes suddenly and there is no time to come to terms with its immediacy. Other factors may prevent the dying person from starting or from completing the tasks of grief. He or she may be too young to do this, or too ill, or be prevented from doing so by not being told about the nearness of his or her death because other people, rightly or wrongly, think this is for the best. There are also tragic circumstances where somebody takes his or her own life, and it is not clear to those who are left to grieve whether the person who died really wanted this to happen. Over the next few chapters we shall be looking more closely at the extra burden of grief which falls on the bereaved when the person who died could not start or finish the major task of grieving for his or her own loss of life.

But where there is time, and the person who is going to die is aware of this, it does not always happen that the last few months of that person's life are used to ease the pain of grieving for the dying person or for those who will be bereaved. The chance may be lost for a variety of reasons. For example, it may be that the dying person cannot accept the full reality of what he or she will lose. It is hard enough to realise every aspect of somebody else's death, let alone our own. And the acceptance of our own death needs to be reconciled with our own need to go on living as long as we can. Many people also refuse help during the early stages of realising that they are going to die soon, because this would force them to accept the truth, and they cannot or will not.

When you are caring for somebody who is going to die, and knows this, failure in any of these acceptance tasks on their part can be heart-breaking for you, particularly if you have completed them. You can find yourself arranging help, only to have it rejected. The dying person may refuse to face facts, and insist on making plans you know cannot be carried out. Worst of all, perhaps, is the agony of feeling how much hurt, how much terror is locked up inside somebody you love, which he or she will not share with you. You have to watch while the suffering from the illness is added to the suffering from an unresolved grief, and there may be nothing you can do to help. The need to go on, where it concerns a person grieving for his or her own life, is often not truly faced, as the need to go on not only into life, but also into death. The old question is avoided, not answered. As a result the dying person bottles up fear and anger, and withdraws from real contact, pretending to be brave, but in reality becoming more isolated than before, or more dependent on other people pretending also that the death will not happen.

Your own death

As we saw when we began our exploration of grief, each one of us can picture the way we would most like to die. Nearly always what we imagine – whether we realise this or not – could only come about if, before we die, we have completed the tasks of grieving for ourselves. We need to have become reconciled with death so that in dying we are not distressed. We need to go on into death as a natural extension of our lives, and to have somebody with us who will not interfere but simply help by being there. If we can do all this we will have completed the acceptance tasks of grief.

At the same time, I believe that when most people talk about the way they would like to die, they also prefer to have resisted both isolation and dependence. For example, although there are many people who say that they want to be alone to die, I have never met anybody who says he or she wants a lonely death. Isolation is something we all want to resist successfully before we die. And the same is true of dependence. There is a widespread horror of being a helpless burden upon other people, and of being no better than a vegetable as we approach death.

If, in your own dying, you can fully realise that you are going to die, and complete your own grieving for yourself, then you can be free to help those whom you will leave behind. The problem is – as we said at the beginning, though not quite in these terms – few deaths are like this. Even if there is time for the dying person to complete his own grief, and to join in the grief of those who will be bereaved, he or she may not be aware fully of what is happening, or may be unable or unwilling either to grieve personally or to share in the grief of others.

A memorial

I believe that we cannot fully appreciate what is involved when somebody dies from a long, incurable illness unless we accept that each person who dies has a need to grieve for his or her own life that will be lost. Unfortunately this need is too seldom recognised. Where it is acknowledged, and respected, a very different situation is created from where it is either not acknowledged or cannot be met by the dying person. Let us look at an example of a death where it was not fully acknowledged and only partially met. I think we can then leave the matter there.

In one sense this book is a memorial to a woman I knew as a

friend and colleague and whom I shall remember with love. Her name was Josie, and she died of cancer. She lived almost at the top of a large block of council flats in Brixton, South London, and she wrote to me one November saying she was lonely and would like to join an organisation I had set up for lonely people, but could not afford even the modest subscription fee we charged. I phoned her, and not long after she became our full-time membership secretary. A few weeks later she discovered she had breast cancer. I could tell many stories about her, but what I want to recount here concerns Josie's struggle to accept her own death without passively giving up her life. Step by step, as she fought her illness, as she realised that she was going to be one of the minority who die from cancer, and as she grieved for her own life, Josie learned – and taught me and other people – how to face all the tasks of grief for herself and for those who knew her. None of us, I think, knew this at the time. We could not have put a name to what we were learning. It is only now, looking back on those years, that I can see clearly what she was doing and what the rest of us were doing. Except perhaps for one man – a wise doctor who worked with her some of the time, and whom I shall not name here, but whose work is known all over the world because of his care and concern for the dying and his research into grief – except for him, I don't think any of us understood.

Like many people who find they have cancer, Josie began by refusing to accept even the reality that there was a lump in her breast. Her life up to that point had contained many problems. She was separated by a gulf of anger and anxiety from anything like honest communication with her former husband, her children, and her mother. She knew from an inner knowledge of herself that she was an intelligent and caring person, but she had scarcely ever experienced a relationship in which more than the tiniest fraction of this truth had been acknowledged and accepted without question. Uncared for, she had often neglected herself. She got drunk easily and often in the lonely privacy of her flat and talked wise-sounding nonsense to herself. The courage to face an investigation of her cancer took months to gather and frequently deserted her. It may be that joining me and my other colleagues, and being recognised as valuable not so much by us as by the other people she helped, gave her enough courage at last. She had a new identity, a new confidence because she was so obviously accepted and liked by the lonely people she met at our meetings. She felt she belonged with them and, as membership secretary, had an important new way of using her experience as a lonely person herself. So one day she jauntily announced that she was going into hospital to have a lump looked at. I doubt if any of us knew at the time how much of an achievement this had been.

When Josie came home she had had a breast removed. Each of us helped in our own way, distressed partly by her feeling that it was she who needed to reassure us and to cheer us up, when we felt it should be the other way round. One woman colleague, I found out later, went to see Josie a day or so after the operation, and gently gave her a bath, to help Josie get used to the new shape. I went with Josie when she was measured for a prosthesis. Subtly, one step at a time, Josie began to build on the care and loving attention she was receiving. And little by little, one after the other, I think we all began to resent this.

Resistance

It was difficult enough to be honest about what was happening at the time, and no easier now. But anger with Josie began to simmer and occasionally to burst out. I think I was not alone in beginning to set limits to the amount of time I gave her, the extent to which I was prepared to listen to her. Maybe she was testing the limits herself. She began to get drunk more often, to phone late at night and talk about her 'pain', saying that nobody understood or tried to understand. Looking back, I know she was right. At the time I, and others, resented what she was saying and rejected it. Maybe we wanted her to feel grateful, or maybe we were threatened by her ruthless honesty in this and other matters. As the months passed, Josie refused to be ignored. She chose her own method of resistance, but it was effective enough to prevent me at least from isolating her into a tidy, predictable corner of my work-life. She would not just be grateful and stop complaining!

At some time during this period I am sure she knew that the mastectomy had not ended her cancer. Perhaps she knew all along. So she began to grieve for her own life. Little by little she gathered courage together to face different aspects of the reality that she was going to die from the disease. Often, I think, those resources proved inadequate and she slipped back into sheer terror or blind fury, crying out for help when the terror struck, but angrily rejecting it when it was offered. She had grown out of the earlier need to comfort other people by now. But when she demanded comfort for herself as her right, she became a strident, aggressive, disagreeable companion, striking out in all directions with unpalatable 'home truths', and then weeping because the people she hurt would not help her. Still she refused to be isolated. She was impossible to ignore. And still she resisted dependence. Any help she was offered had to be on the understanding that she would tell the truth the way she saw it, and not be 'nice' to people so they could feel privately smug at having helped her.

Goodbye

The cancer inside Josie's body grew and spread. Meanwhile I and all my colleagues had other problems which led at last to the organisation having to cease business. Josie's job ended. For a time I lost touch with her. When, some time later, I felt that my own problems were under control again, I phoned her, and she invited me round to that high-rise flat in Brixton with its view of southern London and the potted bush outside on the balcony. Her mother was with her. Both women were at ease with one another. She spoke of her children whom she now saw regularly. She had altered her name back to what it had been before her marriage, realising, in every sense of the word, that the marriage was over. She gave me her diaries painfully compiled during a recent, introductory stay at the hospice where she expected to die. She was tired and in pain, but more at peace than I had ever seen her.

Josie and I talked about her death while I sat next to her mother. She did not want to die. She felt angry that the cancer and its treatment were taking away her independence both physically and emotionally. She wanted to be conscious of her own dying, she told me, to make it something she did for herself. Until that time came she was determined to go on with her life. She resented the nursing care which treated her as a manageable case, a carefully washed and fed specimen of tranquillized, cancerous humanity. But she did not resent death itself. She had accepted it, and would turn it into reality as far as was within her power her way – not theirs, but hers – so that Josie's dying would be as distinctive and unique as Josie herself, and not one whit more or less than this.

I think I said goodbye to her when I left. I remember kissing her mother, and then kissing her. I knew that in one sense saying goodbye was not important, and now I understand why. I realise now as I write this that I am saying goodbye to her, and accepting her goodbye to me by telling her story. She had shared with me the grief she felt at the loss of her own life. She could not have shared anything more important than that.

13

The Unexpected Death

When somebody dies suddenly and unexpectedly, special problems arise for the grieving person which we need to understand. As a result of these, the work of grief can be particularly difficult to start, and in some respects, even harder to complete. Whether your own grieving began this way, or you want to be able to help others to whom it has happened, or if you are aware of your own need to prepare yourself for grief in general, then there are aspects of a grief which starts this way which raise deep and often disturbing questions you will wish to consider.

There are three main points we have to look at. The first of these is that a sudden bereavement generally leaves in its wake a great many practical problems. These can have the effect of delaying the start of the grieving process, because there simply may not be time immediately after the bereavement for anything except economic survival. Even if there is no financial problem, practical matters can keep the bereaved person so busy that part of the shock is itself delayed, and the early realisation stage takes longer than it would have done otherwise. Secondly, an unexpected death often happens without any emotional preparation. We may have to face the sudden loss of somebody we love without ever having discussed death. Also it may be the first death we have had to face, and the one person we need by our side while we live through the enormity of loss is the one we have lost. Thirdly, in any sudden bereavement, we are aware that the person who died will not have had time to grieve on his or her own account. This makes it particularly difficult to accept certain aspects of what has happened to him or her. We may feel the need to grieve not only for our loss, but also in some way to help the one who died by completing that person's grief-work too. This 'double grief' needs to be dealt with too.

Practical problems

When they are faced with the emergency of a sudden bereave-

107

ment, some people find that they are quite unable to deal with the practical problems that arise. Others discover that this is all they can deal with at the start, and that the emotional impact of their loss is delayed. There seems to be no way of predicting in advance which reaction you are likely to have. Some very practical people go through an emotional collapse at the start, and cannot handle practical matters, whilst those who have always thought of themselves as incompetent are surprised at the logical and decisive way they respond to the situation.

In general, shock during the early days helps most people to keep going longer and in a more clear-headed way than they expected. It can help you if shock delays the emotional impact of the bereavement, particularly if you have to deal with complicated arrangements or an immediate financial problem. If you feel better keeping yourself busy, even if there are people around who want you to let them take over, then it is a good idea to insist on being fully occupied. But you also need to recognise you will need to let go sooner or later. The numbness that comes from total exhaustion is not an ally to be trusted for very long.

From the start it can be useful in dealing with practical problems if you are quite ruthless about asking people for help and setting exact limits upon what you want them to do for you. If strangers are approached in this spirit they will usually assist you willingly, partly because then they do not feel so helpless – and you should always tell them why you need help – and partly because, if you set limits, they know where they stand. Neighbours particularly will prefer to know that you are not going to be dependent upon them for very long. What often worries people is that they are afraid of getting involved too deeply, that is to say, committing themselves to short-term help and then finding that they have a major responsibility on their hands.

The exception to this general rule is, of course, money. If you need cash as a result of the emergency, then it is best to ask somebody you know very well, or to approach an official body such as the bank or an appropriate government agency. Friends, relatives, and sometimes neighbours, may say to you, 'If you need any help be sure to ask.' If the help you need is financial, the rule is – ask for advice first rather than cash.

In deciding what to do about practical problems, it can help you to be aware of the feelings you are likely to go through in the early stages of a sudden bereavement. You can expect, for example, to find yourself full of doubt about whether you have enough money to survive, even though there had been no doubt about this only the day before you were bereaved. This is part of the normal reaction particularly where the person you have lost was the 'breadwinner' of the family, or where you may have to suffer some short-term financial loss due to time away from work. So you need to beware of over-reacting, and to try not to worry more than is precisely necessary about your finances. Also, if the person you have lost was away from home when the death occurred, you can expect to feel a need to be with him or her, even though this may create considerable practical difficulties for yourself and others. In deciding what to do, it may help you to delay a final decision for a while, particularly if you feel instinctively or impulsively that you must act straight away.

One very practical need which you may not be aware of is the need you have to take care of yourself during the early stages. Keeping yourself busy is one thing. Neglecting your own health is yet another. Not only does self-neglect add to your own difficulties, but it is also often a disguised cry for help directed at the people around you. It would be better to ask for help, rather than place other people in the position where they feel obliged to give it to you unwillingly or out of a sense of duty. These may be hard words, but remember that increasing your dependence upon others could lessen your chances of independence later. So use some of your energy, however little you have, and whatever immediate practical demands there are upon it, to plan some rest for yourself, and to ensure that you can stay clean and tidy. It may seem only a trivial point, but it can make all the difference to how you feel and what you are capable of doing in the trying days that lie ahead of you.

The emotional impact

Where there is a sudden and unexpected death, there is also a special need for the grieving person and all those concerned with helping him or her, to understand what the immediate impact is likely to be. We have already looked at the earliest reactions in describing the way Joyce heard of her husband's death, and the pattern of realisation which is central to the process of grief has been mentioned many times. What we need to do now is to look at some of the ways these early reactions are often misunderstood and mishandled, usually because of ignorance or unthinking insensitivity, rather than malice on anybody's part.

One fairly common problem is that it is often thought unwise to leave somebody unaccompanied during the early stages in case they 'do something silly' – a euphemism for committing suicide. There is, of course, no harm in making sure that somebody who is shocked or emerging from shock has somebody else nearby, and it can be a great help. But it is often done clumsily, and for the wrong reasons.

The bereaved person is usually unlikely to hurt himself or herself, and certainly does not want to be treated like an invalid or to be over-protected. Somebody who will behave calmly and normally, who will not be alarmed by emotional discharge, such as compulsive talking, violent, or prolonged but quiet weeping, withdrawal into trance-like states, or out-or-time behaviour such as starting the washing in the middle of the night – somebody who can accept this kind of thing without over-reacting, will be far more useful than any self-appointed guardian or warder.

The need of the bereaved person to express doubt and to ask questions which may already have been answered is also often handled ineptly, particularly when the person asking triggers uncomfortable feelings that other people were suppressing. For example, a grieving person may not have been told the whole truth, to 'protect' his or her feelings. So what has apparently happened does not make sense. However uncomfortable the truth may be – that there were very severe physical injuries, that there was a great deal of pain, or whatever – it is surely better for it to be told openly and faced, than for the grieving person to be manipulated by dishonesty and to have found out later when the life-death crisis might be much closer. This kind of half-truth manipulation is also, unfortunately, often seen as the best way to deal with a child's grief. It is the worst way. Adults in my opinion have an even greater obligation to be honest with children over grief than they have with their fellow adults. Children whose grief goes unregarded, who are misled and puzzled, or whose natural reactions to adult grief are suppressed, will often delay their grief indefinitely, and lose some of their ability to deal with such feelings permanently. When they face their severest crisis later as adults they will start with a major disadvantage as a result.

Wild threats

As the grieving person struggles to comprehend what has happened, and fails many times during the early stages of grief, he or she will experience very strong feelings. We have already seen how the response to strong doubt, and to an overwhelming urge to question and requestion can be dealt with badly. This also applies to the intense feelings which are associated with the insecurity phase of realisation. These feel-ings – basically anger or fear, or the two combined together as worry – are often expressed violently, not because the person is ordinarily a violent person, but because the feelings are too intense to be controlled. It does not help the grieving person if those around are shocked or alarmed by this. For example, in your own early reactions if you experience a sudden loss, you might need to express violent anger against the person who has died. This is something you honestly feel, and need to express. It is only part of what you feel. But you will not be helped by well-meaning people who tell you that you do not really feel this way.

Anger can also come out as fury over little things – the way funeral arrangements have been made, minor irritations with other people's mannerisms, a chance remark that is innocent enough but might be taken as inept criticism, insensitivity or cynicism. This also can produce a kind of chain-reaction as other people have their own suppressed grief-anger ignited, and there may be considerable fuss. It probably helps if you can avoid rows of this kind, but once they have started they usually do a great deal of good in ventilating feelings and clearing the air. They are probably the reason for the almost normal phenomenon of the post-bereavement family row. If their causes are fully recognised and accepted they do no harm. If not they can lead to permanent, institutionalised splits in families. Almost every family has had at least one such schism in its history.

You may also find yourself needing to express anger against yourself, by saying, for example, that you hate yourself and would be better off dead. Fear can also come out in remarks to the effect that you want to run away and have nothing to do with the whole situation ever again. If your feelings are not fully recognised, or such remarks provoke an over-reaction or misunderstanding, you may need to repair the damage later. The way to do this is first, to accept that you said what you felt, and that you are entitled to react this way to your grief. Secondly, however, it was probably more expressive of how intensely you felt, than descriptive of your real intentions. Thirdly, it helps you if you can acknowledge why people over-react to wild threats or violent outbursts. It is because they have their own need to feel angry or afraid or worried or hurt. So when you feel calm again, the best thing you can do is probably not to apologise, but rather to be a good listener to the people who over-reacted and help them come to terms with their feelings. In future, they may be better equipped to help both you and themselves.

We all have our own methods of expressing and dealing with intense fear or anger – violent verbal outbursts directed at ourselves or others, physical outbursts in the form of hitting or breaking inanimate objects, hitting ourselves, violent physical movements, threatening people by shouting, by looking very angry, even by attacking people physically. Grief can make it harder for us to control such reactions, and it is helpful at times to recognise this. We are usually aware of the ways we use, and we can, if necessary, explain them to the people we might alarm or hurt. What is often harder for people to deal with is not so much anger alone, or fear alone, as worry.

Dealing with worry

Worry is often hard for people to understand. It is caused by a combination of fear and anger. When you are worried about something, you tend to swing between the two feelings – for example, being angry that you have a duty to do something you do not want to do, then feeling afraid of what will happen if you don't, then angry again as you feel like refusing, and fearful once more, perhaps about what other people will think of you, then angry with them because of this . . . and so on and on. Violent worry – the sort many grieving people go through in the early stages after a sudden bereavement – is characterised by more violent changes of mood. You swing from anger to fear and back again more often – sometimes so quickly that you literally do not know what you feel. It is also likely that you cannot deal with this in your usual way, by trying successfully to not-worry.

There is no easy answer to this problem. Perhaps the best you can do is to ask a friend who is a good listener to help you by selective listening. This means asking the friend to choose either the things you feel angry about, and ask you questions about this whilst ignoring the things that you are afraid of or anxious about, or, alternatively, ask you only about the matters that provoke a fear response whilst ignoring any signs of anger or frustration you might display. The point of this procedure is that it might help you to break the log-jam caused by feeling equal amounts of intense fear and intense anger. But much will depend on the communication skills of the friends you choose, and a trained counsellor is clearly a better person to turn to for help, even though you may only need this on a short-term basis.

The need to cry

The need to cry has also been mentioned earlier. There are two ways in which this need is commonly misunderstood. Holding back tears is sometimes said to be bad for a person, whilst others will urge you to control yourself – especially, if you happen to be a man. Certainly there are times when it is best to cry freely and without control, and times when it is better to control your tears and stop yourself from weeping. You will be the best judge of what is appropriate. In general, perhaps, weeping is best controlled when it might stop you from making a decision, or might be frightening to a child. It is best to get it out uncontrolled when you feel safe. But there can be no hard and fast rule. We weep for many reasons – from anger or fear, from relief or pleasure, from love, from pity. The worst reason for not weeping is that somebody other than a child might not understand.

Being unprepared

If this is the first time you have encountered death, and if you have never thought about it before, then I think I can assume that you will not have reached this part of the book without having worked quite hard on your grief during the last few months, and certainly since you began to read about grief during the last few days. You will probably also have discovered that your feelings ebb and flow, sometimes being very intense, and at other times hardly being there at all. There may also be times when you feel completely disassociated from your own feelings, as if you were watching yourself from outside your body, looking down from a high position. These feelings need not cause you any anxiety. They are due mainly to your body's need to adjust to a dramatic and painful change in who you are. Early adjustment is often erratic. The human 'system' – body, behaviour, and all other aspects of personality – frequently adapts to violent change by first over-reacting and then under-reacting. The strong feelings followed by weak feelings are a reflection of this, and the 'out-of-the-body' experiences are almost certainly a reaction to the stress caused by all that has happened to you recently.

On a more general point about being prepared for grief, it is worth noting that no way exists of really being prepared for some grief experiences. The shock of a totally unexpected bereavement is something that none of us is ever ready for. We none of us know how we will react if it should happen. Perhaps the only thing that can be said with any certainty is that the greater the shock, the more likely it is that the work of grieving is harder to start. It may not be delayed for very long. Once it starts there is no reason to suppose it is any more difficult than for anybody else, prepared or unprepared, before or after bereavement – and that is difficult enough.

Double grieving

When we suddenly lose somebody we love, particularly if we are not there at the time, we can find that we have two griefs to deal with. We need to adapt to our own loss by carrying out and completing the tasks of grief, and this is essentially a 'self-centred' – though not a 'selfish' – process. The reality to

114

which we have to adapt is our own day-to-day real world, the one in which we have been left alone by the bereavement. When we come up against the crisis, and have to decide the extent of our need to go on despite what has happened or even because of this, then it is our own life and future which we are concerned with, the life and the future of our own 'self'. When we decide about help, we are faced with the need to test how far we should help ourselves or seek help for ourselves – not for anybody else. In resisting isolation and dependence we are, in different ways, asserting our right to be ourselves.

But we may also feel a need to come to terms with the fact that the person who died was not prepared to die, and yet had no choice. This grief is 'other-centred', rather than self-centred. The tasks of grieving, which that other person would have tackled, and which through our love for that person would have been shared, are uncompleted. We may feel a very profound need to carry out not only our own grief-work, but also to grieve on behalf of the other person too.

Let us look at some examples of this in relation to the two main acceptance tasks. We have already considered in depth what is involved when you try to accept the reality of your own loss. In addition to this, when somebody dies suddenly, the grieving person may often find himself trying to feel the loss experienced by the one who died. After a death from illness, grieving is quite commonly accompanied by real and painful symptoms which are very similar or even identical to those of the fatal illness. When this happens there is usually no organic basis for the symptoms, but they should nevertheless be taken seriously and not be 'laughed off' or 'explained away'. After a violent death, from an accident perhaps, the grieving person may also experience great physical pain with no apparent physical cause. Again, the pain is real, and requires treatment appropriate to the pain, even if there may be apparently nothing physical to treat.

In medical circles, such physical manifestations of double grieving are considered to be quite rare, but this may be because they fade away quite quickly and are therefore not reported to doctors. There are, however, other equally distressing ways in which a grieving person can find himself or herself taking on the task of accepting the reality of a death on behalf of the person who was lost. Sometimes, for example, it becomes almost impossible to stop imagining what it must have been like for that person to die. This may happen in dreams or in day-dreams, or seem to become a kind of obsessive need to feel all the pain and terror of that particular death. The re-living of this on behalf of the grieved-for person can be understood as a way of taking over that person's grief at dying, and attempting to accept the full reality of it for him or her.

A pale reflection of such grieving often surfaces in casual conversation years later when people wonder how it must have felt for that person. And bits of it can also come up in the way somebody might make 'at least' statements – such as 'at least he did not suffer any pain' or 'at least she was not left crippled for the rest of her life'. When such statements are made, they commonly sound casual yet cover up a great deal of intense feeling. The people who make them are clearly reassuring themselves in some way, but they often do not sound convinced that what 'at least' happened really did happen. I think they are expressing a need to comfort the person who died as well as themselves, and, in a real sense, to help that person accept the reality of death.

The knowledge that somebody we love has died suddenly without accepting death, perhaps fighting it in vain, or having no chance to fight it at all, is extremely disturbing. In our own grief, accepting the need to go on is likely to be tested by a major crisis. If we try to do this part of the grief-work of our missing loved-ones, we may find ourselves wishing we could have died instead. This feeling is usually very intense, but it is also quite separate from the crisis of our grief. The need to grieve on behalf of companions – people who died in wartime, for example, or people who were killed in an accident which the grieving person survived – is often expressed by taking over the task of accepting and trying to realise for them their need to die willingly. The survivors say, 'I should have died instead.' They wonder why they survived and their companions did not, but this is no casual wondering. Behind it lies a profound need to feel acceptance of death on their behalf, since they were deprived of this. We seldom feel this way about people who died peacefully and knew what was happening to them.

It seems likely that grief on behalf of somebody, as opposed to grief at the loss of somebody, is most likely to occur when the bond between the two people was very strong – either a love relationship or the deep companionship which comes from shared, deeply felt experience, which is very close to love. Certainly I have only met this kind of double grieving where there has been such a bond. The need to do two sets of grieving is understandable where there is such a bond, since the person who survives and the lost partner will have been used to sharing emotionally important tasks. The grieving person in my experience is usually unaware, at a conscious level, of grieving on behalf of somebody else, and of the double burden of grief that is being carried. But there are times when people feel ready to lessen their load, and to let go of the responsibility they are carrying for their lost loved ones or companions. Then they can be helped to explore their feelings, and to realise that they can safely cope only with their own grief.

14

Grief After Suicide

All grief is hard to deal with, but few people would deny that grief for somebody who has committed suicide must be one of the most difficult. The purpose of this chapter is to discuss some of the problems. Even if your grief did not start this way, understanding the nature of grief after suicide can be of use to you not only in helping other people, but also in facing up to some of your own inner feelings about living and dying. And it needs to be said also that if you have ever lost somebody close to you because he or she took the step of suicide, then you will know already how difficult it is to get the special help you know you need. Despite the fact that nearly everybody at some time in his or her life, contemplates killing himself or herself, when somebody close to you actually does this, everybody else seems to enter into a conspiracy of silence. After most deaths they will let you talk, even if they feel uncomfortable. After a suicide people, in general, will not even let you talk.

After a sudden death, we start our grief by feeling exactly the same towards that person as we did when we thought he or she was still alive. And in grief before death, when we know somebody is going to die, we can often improve the relationship before bereavement so that when the death occurs, we can continue to feel good about the person who died. With the majority of suicides, however, there has nearly always been some severe breakdown of communication between the person who took his or her own life, and those who grieve. Grief begins in the context of this fraught relationship. So we will need to look at this and to discuss what might have happened and what can be done about it.

Secondly, there is a sense in which the manner of every person's dying says something about how he or she lived. This is a disturbing thought, and one I do not want to take too far here, but it often seems to me that those who die suddenly often turn out to have been the people who frequently took risks with their health, or were used to being unpredictable rather than cautious. Those who die at peace are often people who lived at peace, either selfishly with themselves, or

118

generously with others. But suicide is probably never that kind of a dying. When you take your own life, you are saying something about that life, and you are usually saying it to those who will grieve for you. Deciding what somebody meant by dying is extremely difficult when they have not told us, and this can be especially hard to live with after a suicide. It can also, of course, lead to what we have called 'double grieving', and this is another area of difficulties we need to explore.

Kinds of suicide

All suicides are different, and we need to start by looking systematically at some of the main ways people choose to commit the act, so we can draw some general conclusions about what they might be saying to those who will care what happens.

In my own work with people who talk of suicide, and with people who grieve after suicide, I have come to the conclusion that there are basically two kinds. One kind is really a statement of anger, and the other is an expression of fear. Let us look first at examples of 'anger' suicide.

Anger suicide

Not everybody is able to experience the feelings of extreme rage, mainly because some of us are taught from babyhood to suppress this strong, destructive feeling. But if you have ever been consumed by intense anger, then you will know how this is so often expressed when the feeling starts to get beyond control, by you attacking your own body. You might feel an urge to cut your body, perhaps to hack away part of it, to slash at it or cut it into small pieces. Ordinarily these urges fade as soon as you become fully aware of them, and you turn them into something less drastic. But the feelings are real enough, and are not an uncommon part of normal rage. Other similar impulses might make you feel like crushing your body, of letting it be crushed. You might want to smash parts of yourself. Rage is often made worse, also, by feeling that people around you who ought to care about you are refusing to understand how strong your emotion is. Also, when they are the cause of the problem, you might want to hurt them, and

119

only when you cannot do this do the destructive urges get turned in upon yourself.

People who attack their own bodies fatally in such ways seem to me to be expressing anger. To slash or cut your own body, to force it to be crushed or broken, to throw it away so that it is smashed like a discarded piece of rubbish, is to make a violent statement about the value of that body and the life it contains. It seems often also to be an expression of an anger that the person concerned had been unable fully to communicate to those who matter, and has tried to contain and bottle up, but which now bursts out with volcanic force. Frustration is anger that is suppressed. The anger suicide demonstrates that suppression has failed, that only one way is left to show people the truth about how much anger was there. If the effect is messy and horrifying, if it causes distress to those who are affected, then this is only a fraction of the messiness, the horror, the distress, the anger that the person committing the act felt. They will never understand, those who ought to care – that is the message. Even if I kill myself like this, they will never understand. But at least I can make them see a small part of what they have done to me, so that they suffer too, like they have made me suffer.

We do not need to go into the deep psychology of self-mutilation to understand the kind of feelings that lead to this type of death. But we do need to recognise that it is a shout of total anger, the ultimate scream of rage, and that it is intended to be heard. If somebody has, in effect, screamed and shouted at you in this way as part of your relationship then this will not be the first time you have had shouts and screams of uncontrollable anger directed at you from that person, although none has been quite so extreme before. In your heart you know this is true. It will take all your courage to begin the tasks of grief starting from such a rejection of yourself by one whom you wanted to love more. Or maybe you can recognise in the turbulent history of your relationship that your grieving for what might have been began long before this final shout of hatred. After such a death, those who grieve are forced to re-examine all that went before, and to face the reality of what had been lost not by the death itself, but by the relationship with the one who died.

Fear suicide

Some of the people who make successful suicide attempts have probably given up being angry, and have decided that nobody knows or cares even that they exist. Theirs is an extreme form of retreat from life, a final running away and abandonment of being. They do not damage their bodies, so much as release themselves from corporeal existence. To continue with life, with the pain and hopelessness of it all, is more than they have the courage to bear. They have been anxious and afraid so often that the fear of being alive becomes at last greater than the fear of death. In your own experience of strong fear, you will have known the feeling of not wanting to be here, of wanting to be anywhere else but living this life in this way, at this time, in this place. When there is nowhere else to escape to, you can come to believe that only the ultimate escape is open to you – the escape into endless oblivion through being dead. Anger – the first response – is something you cannot feel in this state of mind. All you feel is the flight response, the strongest expression of which is a flight for ever from being alive.

Fear suicide is designed to leave the body behind as an empty shell. The methods chosen, therefore, tend to be bloodless, like a tidying-up of the shell before departure, rather than a damaging of it. Self-poisoning, through overdoses of pre-scribed tablets or by gassing are the most common. Self-drowning is probably a similar kind of suicide.

The statement implied in this kind of death – and often left behind in a written message for those whom it might concern – is frequently self-denigratory, far more one of sorrow than of anger. It expresses an inability to go on any longer. Life has become a burden, and the person feels that it is better to end that life rather than inflict it on anybody else. Those who are left behind are being told, in effect, that they will be better off without the person who dies, that they too will be released from having to care, just as the victim will be released from care.

Sometimes the victim wants people left behind to be sad they did not care enough, maybe to feel as miserable and as lonely as the victim, and through this to understand what has been done. But the fear suicide is a way of forcing people to be

121

anxious, rather than angry, to miss somebody they did not love enough, rather than to be hurt by somebody whom they did not seem to love at all. It seems to say – you have forgotten me while I was alive, and I challenge you by my death to go on forgetting me.

If somebody close to you has chosen this way of dying, then you will know that he or she had said this to you before on more than one occasion – that you would be better off without him or her, that you did not really understand and could not give the care that was needed. There will have been other withdrawals into a misery that was too much for you to bear, other retreats from contact, such as long periods of not-speaking, or times when the person seemed unable to let you get near however much anxiety you showed. And there will be times when you gave up trying perhaps because you could not continue hiding the anger you felt, but mainly because you could no longer live the life you wanted as long as he or she was there as a desperately sad responsibility. At such times – long before the death – you were already trying to face the realities of the relationship, so you could have a life of your own. Grief will have begun then, though you may not have recognised it as such.

Shock

Like other kinds of sudden death, suicide is often a cause of major shock, and in both cases the shock is usually worse if the one who will most need to grieve is the first to know what has happened. For this reason, much of what was said earlier about unexpected loss applies equally to the aftermath of suicide. Once the first part of the shock has worn off, there are practical problems to deal with, and an emotional impact that may be delayed, but which those who have the immediate care of the bereaved need to understand.

The best way to look at this is in terms of the grief-work that has to be done. The same three major tasks of acceptance need to be tackled, and the same two tasks of resistance. As with any grief, realisation takes place in the form of making new sense of the relationship between the grieving person and the one who has died. With a suicide, your first task is to accept the reality that your relationship was not working well

122

for either of you, and that this happens between many people, just as badly, even where the one who dies does not kill himself or herself. It was the choice of the dead person to make a dramatic public statement about this, and not your choice. You are entitled to feel angry about this for many reasons, and it will help you from the start to feel and express some of this anger.

Helplessness

How do you begin to accept the reality of your loss? First, as with any death, it may be difficult to accept the reality that he or she is dead. But this is also complicated by the need to accept what he or she did. With an anger suicide there is usually no doubt that the person meant to die. People who kill themselves from anger leave no room for any last minute reprieves, and if they tell somebody in advance, they generally make sure that intervention will be far too late to prevent the death. But fear suicide often looks as though it was not really meant to succeed. It often looks like the 'cry for help' that went tragically wrong. So you may find great difficulty in deciding whether he or she really meant to die, and be filled with anxiety in case you could actually have been there in time to save the person from death. Under these circumstances perhaps the hardest truth to accept is that it doesn't ultimately make much difference whether you could have been there or not. The person who died wanted you to be anxious and to feel helpless. You were expected to feel responsible, but to fail – as so many times before in so many different ways. The death that looks as though it was a 'cry for help' that went wrong was an act designed without your consent to make you feel guilty. So you have a choice. You can feel guilty if that is what you want, or you can feel angry that you were not consulted, and not really expected to be of any use.

Feelings of guilt are often associated with suicide. So we need to understand about guilt. It is really self-punishment. Whenever we feel guilty we are hurting ourselves, usually because we think we have done something that 'deserves' punishment. Guilt is something we learn, usually in early childhood. It begins as part of the apparatus of parental control, because a child who punishes himself saves the parent time and trouble. For example, the child who is made to feel guilty may benefit because it pleases the parent, and takes the heat off the child. But there was probably no need for this heat in the first place. Making you feel guilty in childhood, then, was a way of manipulating you. Your feelings of guilt are probably triggered mostly by people who are the present-day equivalent of parents, either because you feel responsible to them, or responsible for them.

The fact of the matter is that when the person died you were not able to help. However hard it may be to accept this it is still a fact. The death was designed in such a way as to leave you helpless to intervene. Punishing yourself about this is not going to change the facts. And you now have a new choice about whether you want to be manipulated into feeling guilty. Realising that you may have been manipulated by this person many times in the past may take a long time, or you may know it already. Either way, you punishing yourself will not help him or her now. And you need to think very clearly about whether it will help you. Then you need to tell somebody who, unlike your childhood superiors, will have no vested interest in making judgements about your behaviour.

Responsibility

Each one of us goes through times in life when we are responsible for other people. As children we may be made to feel responsible for our parents' well-being, and we may carry important parts of this responsibility with us for the rest of our lives. In our love relationships with other adults we tend to repeat aspects of the same sense of responsibility we learned from them, modelling a large part of our ways of responding to one another on the way our parents dealt with us, and with one another. When we become parents ourselves, we take responsibility for our children, and the way we treat them is often a compromise between the way we were aware of being dealt with – and can either avoid if we did not like it, or improve upon if we did – and the unconscious imitation of their methods of bringing up a child. But there is a limit to responsibility.

What is this limit? It must be one of the hardest things in the world to define, but I think we have to accept ultimately that we cannot be responsible for the life of somebody who is able to take that life and does so. At a certain stage in the normal development of the person, he or she becomes old enough to end his or her life as a way of resolving crisis. It is that person's right to do this. We can, it seems to me, never take away that right, even though we may decide to prevent the person from being able to exercise the right in order to protect him or her. But once we do this, we have created a power relationship between ourselves and that person. We have made him or her dependent upon us. We have also given that person the power to threaten us – to threaten suicide so that we dare not end the relationship and relinquish our power over that person for fear of failing. The result is that the two of us are locked into the classic power relationship of jailer and warder. Both are equally prisoners.

This is what so often seems to happen when there is an angry suicide. It also seems to be one of the characteristics of those immensely tangled relationships which lead to the long suicide of serious drug addiction. Untangling the truth about what really happened, and facing the reality of it, is a task which requires almost superhuman courage and honesty. I do not believe it can be done without expert help. But the first step towards recovery is usually acceptance of the fact that there was a power relationship, not a loving relationship. Then it can be realised that power and love are not compatible. Somewhere along the line, the person who died and the person who grieves stopped loving one another and began fighting one another. The grief for what-might-have-been started then, often long before death took place. That is the proper place for the grief to start, and there will always be signs that it did so. Those who can be helped to see this and to reach a realistic understanding of what they were doing, can be helped to accept that their loss began long ago. They can then start to take responsibility for their own grief, and to accept that the one who died has already taken responsibility – however negatively and destructively, for the grief he or she felt when the relationship turned from one of love to one of power.

Whether it was an anger suicide or a fear suicide, the acceptance of reality, and the acceptance of the need to go on, are almost impossible to start without this recognition that what needs to be grieved for is the love that died, and not the person who died. Double grieving, trying to do that person's grief-work as well as your own will not help you. Indeed, if you look back over the last phase of the relationship, then you may be able to see that before he or she died you were already trying to get the person to accept realities, to accept the need to go on, to seek help, to resist isolation, to fight against dependence. You were, in fact, trying to do that person's grief-work then. You did all you could. The work is over now for him or her. Now you must look to your own life, and carry out your own grief tasks.

Dependence and isolation

So it is up to you to seek help for yourself, to decide whether to be hurt permanently by the last act of a free individual or not. It may be a fitting memorial that you should never be truly alive in your own right. This option is yours, and you will take it into the crisis of grief, and, like the one who died before you, decide how to exercise your own freedom, and the control you have at last over your own life. If you are grieving for somebody who died an angry death, then maybe you will still want to have the last word in your power struggle. If your grief is for somebody whose fear was too great to be lived with, then you can choose to react the same way to your own fear.

If you do not decide to die, but do not decide either to live more fully than before, then for the rest of your life you will be isolated by dependence upon somebody who no longer exists in any real sense of the word. But if you face the crisis and come through, you will have before you nothing more or less than the grief that awaits anybody else who is bereaved – with all its pain and difficulty.

15

When a Child Dies

Every grief has its own special problems, and most of them, as we have seen, arise from the nature of the relationship we have with the person who dies. There may be destructive feelings which remain hidden – feelings of anger or fear, normal in many of the ways we relate to one another, but which are suppressed to keep an artificial peace, as in many marriages or adult relationships. Sometimes these feelings burst out, and in a few tragic cases can be so intense that they ultimately receive public expression in suicide. Or feelings may be open and loving, particularly if the person who dies can do his or her grief-work first, helped by the loving support of those who are most closely concerned.

To understand the special grief we have when a child of our own dies, we need to look at the special features of the child-parent relationship. This relationship is, to some extent, capable of being like any other between two people who have a similar experience of a shared world – anything from an intimate, deeply valued friendship, to something akin to respectful strangership. But although this part of the relationship might be attainable by any two people who meet and become close, there are feelings we have towards our own children which arise only because of our parenthood. These are the feelings we need to look at here, because the hurt of grief without them would be no easier and no harder to bear than with the loss of any other person to whom we feel close.

A special relationship

What is it that makes your own child different in your eyes from any other category of person? Obviously one very important factor is that as its natural parent you contributed half of the genetic material from which that person grew. So the two of you will share many physical characteristics. You are likely to look like one another, and there will also be similarities between your own child and your parents and grandparents. You are likely to have a very similar set of physical capabilities too. For example your child is likely to have a similar degree of dexterity to your own. There is a fifty-fifty chance that it will have the same capacity you have for physical endurance – whether this is great or small. In a biological sense the two of you are part of the same life-stream.

You are also quite likely to behave in similar ways. There is no need to use a genetic theory to explain this. My own belief is that all our behaviour is learned, and none of it is inherited. This is why we can, at almost any time in our lives, learn to behave differently from our parents. But when we look at the way people learn, we can see that they can only do what their bodies will allow them to do, and since your child has most of the same physical limitations and capabilities you have, he or she will, at the start, be restricted to learning to do similar things to you. For example, two faces that are alike can only make the same range of facial expressions. Two voices that are similar are going to be limited to much the same repertoire of sounds.

The child learns to be like its parents because its opportunities to learn are, for a significant part of its life, controlled precisely by the environment they provide and the 'rules' they follow themselves as to how every tiny element in that environment is to be used. Each new bit of the child's behaviour becomes part of its personality. And, unless it breaks the 'rules', or learns from somebody other than a natural parent, its behaviour will be like that of either or both its parents not only because its physical equipment is similar, but also because they control what it learns on, and how it learns.

Special feeling

What does all this contribute to the special feeling we have for a child of our own? First of all, it means that the child begins as physically part of us. Its very first environment is the space in its mother's body where it is conceived and grows, and that cannot happen without the presence of sperm from the father. Usually both have thought about having a baby, and both take responsibility from the start for protecting it. They work together to provide an environment so it can grow and thrive inside the mother. They decide where and how they want it to be born, and they prepare the environment in which it will grow through babyhood, childhood, and adolescence, into mature adulthood. They are looking after a part of themselves, and the way they do this will be a direct reflection of the way each of them feels about himself or herself. They are also looking after a part of one another, so how each feels about the other partner is also reflected in how he or she feels about the baby.

The responsibility a parent feels towards himself or herself, as a 'good' or 'bad' mother or father varies from person to person. Some people are brought up to believe that parenting is very difficult, and are terrified of making mistakes. Yet others apparently sail through it without a care in the world. And there are also wide variations in the extent to which parents are made to feel responsible to their own parents or parents-in-law, with some intervening often and others never interfering.

The expectations a parent has of his or her own child also varies widely. At one extreme there are fathers who see their child from conception onwards as 'following in their own footsteps', or as playing the father's favourite sport as a star member of the national team. At the other extreme there are fathers and mothers who seem totally indifferent to what their child will grow up to be or to do. But it is the more subtle expectations of the parents for the child that last longest and have the most influence on their relationship. Nearly all parents are deeply convinced that their children need to be controlled so they will grow up fitted for a similar place in the world. It is not enough for a boy to become a man. He is expected to become a certain kind of man, and there are sanctions to stop him turning into the 'wrong' sort of male. Girls are trained to meet their parents' expectations also – so they do not grow into the 'wrong' sort of woman. They will be 'corrected' if they show signs of not being 'good' girls, 'good' daughters, potentially 'good' wives and mothers. In practice, 'good' always means some idealised version of 'just like me'. To fit them for a similar place in the world, parents want their children to learn the skills and customs they see as appropriate to that place, or, if they want something better for them, appropriate to a superior life-style. Some expectations are expressed as 'hopes' for their children, and, when they are not met, as disappointments. The whole pattern of child care varies according to the kind of sanctions used, and the severity with which they are applied. But expectations are nearly always part of the picture.

When a child dies

What then do we grieve for when a child of our own dies? If we are lucky enough or wise enough to get to know that child as a person in his or her own right, then we grieve for the loss of that person. Such a grief is no easier and no harder than grieving for any other person whom we have known intimately, and loved deeply. It will take all the courage we have to complete it. We will always love and miss the person we have lost. He or she was a complete person in his or her own right, somebody who had realised all the potential he or she could, and who then died. We can call him or her by name and say goodbye whenever we want to. There is a reality about that person's life which we can accept, and a value to it which we can realise.

If you have lost a child shortly before it was born, then this does not mean to say you never knew that child. You probably knew what its name was to be, and when it was born and its sex became known, it had a right to be called ever after by that name. So you have somebody to say goodbye to – a person who lived as well as he or she could for as long as he or she could. I hope you saw your baby, too. He or she was real, and the death was real. If you saw your baby, this is easier to accept. I hope also that you went to your baby's funeral – both of you together. Fathers and mothers have an equal need to grieve, and an equal right to grieve, because they have both lost an equally valuable reality. If your child lived to be a baby, and died as one, then all this applies to you too: your child was a person, and you have lost that person.

Sometimes a child dies who is old enough to understand death in his or her own way. If such a child dies suddenly, without time to grieve for the life he or she will lose, then, if you knew him or her as a real person, you will grieve over that loss. It will be a hard loss to bear, but the tasks of grief will enable you to accept the reality, to ask for the help you need, to add to your own life-commitment through crisis, and to avoid the isolation of feeling that nobody can ever understand

130

why you are still dependent upon the person who is no longer there as a living part of your life. Nothing will make that grief easy, and it will be no easier or no harder than grieving after any sudden, unexpected, and tragic loss. If there is time to help your child to understand that he or she will die, then those of you most closely concerned can work with that child in an open and loving way so that you tackle the tasks of grief together. Your child is already a person, and has been for a long time. Now, if you have never really met as equals before, it is surely right to do so. You will need to talk openly and honestly about what will happen, and to admit ignorance of the things you do not know about. There will be no need for long solemn lectures. Just take the casual opportunities that arise naturally, and answer the questions he or she asks without fuss. This will help both of you to accept the reality of what will be lost.

Remember the realisation process, for children use it too. There will be doubt and questioning, fear and anger and worry to deal with lovingly and matter-of-factly as well. There will be ways also in which the dying person tests your loyalty, your willingness to accept that he or she still belongs as part of your life despite the coming death. As well as all this, each little bit of realisation will show him or her as different from other people. You need to help your child to see that this difference is special and valuable to you, and that he or she can accept this difference as real and important.

A child who is grieving for his or her own life, just like an adult doing this, needs to accept the need to go on as long as possible in a full commitment to life, and only to accept death when there is no alternative. When the child tests this through crisis, you must be there, and help in any way you can. There are no rules for this kind of help. All you can do is follow your feelings. But you will also face your own crises of commitment. These are your responsibility, not the dying person's. Resolve them for yourself. It may be tempting to transfer responsibility to the child – to say that you are only living because your child needs you. This would be cruel and quite untrue.

Your child will need help that you cannot give. This is his or her right as a complete person. Relationships that he or she makes may seem at times to be very like your own parental

131

relationship. It is easy to be jealous. Hard though it may be, remember that if you are possessive, you will be trespassing on your child's right to be a free person, and to grieve in his or her own way. Face this need in yourself. Take it into crisis, or ask for help while you talk it through. In reality you do not own your child, and it will help you to realise every last aspect of this fact.

As your child nears his or her death, there will probably be an increased physical dependence upon you. Try, however, to reduce emotional dependence, and to let the dying person have more and more of his or her own feelings. If yours are different, say so, as one stranger might to another, not to make the child feel the way you do, but to show you are both independently important. Encourage social independence in the form of visits from friends your child would like to see. And be careful about becoming dependent yourself upon the child's illness. If it is your only purpose in life, then you are in danger of needing it. Keep your sense of fun, and your ability to be loved by other people, actively alive. Stay sexual. It will take courage to find the beauty that is all round you, but you know you have that courage. And staying independent from the illness, instead of coming to rely on it as an excuse for not having a life of your own, will add to your strength. It will also help you to resist isolation. Never be in a position to say that nobody but you really understands. If this is true for more than a few hours, then you will have failed to accept your own needs, and have missed the chance to help others understand. It is the first step towards delayed grief. Death, when it comes, will be sad and difficult, like all deaths for those with whom we have grieved in advance.

Responsibility

The problem with so much grief people experience after the death of a child is that the parent never took the opportunities that were there during the child's lifetime to get to know him or her as an equally complete person who just happened to be at a different stage of development. I think this is a tragedy in itself – a tragedy whether a child dies or lives. But we have to accept realistically that many of us are brought up with too little love, and subject to too much power. This leads us to accept distorted and disturbed relationships as normal. I have written elsewhere about the wider effects of this, and the way our relationships break down so often in bouts of uncontrollable unhappiness, and I have said there what I believe we can do about this. (In *How to Cope With Your Nerves*, Sheldon Press.) This is not the place to take the point any further.

What I think we have to accept is that when a parent saw his or her child mainly as a responsibility and not so much as a person, then the death will be experienced in part at least as a failure of responsibility. Some of it is felt quite needlessly as guilt. Some is directed outwards towards other people who were seen as having more responsibility, and gets experienced as blame. Both types of feeling nearly always get suppressed, and the death of the child produces further reduction in the life-commitment of the parents. If you feel guilt at the loss of a baby, as a miscarriage, a stillbirth, or after the birth, then please seek the help of a fully qualified counsellor.

Expectations

It often happens also that when a child dies, disappointed expectations go underground. They are usually unrealistic, and help the disappointed person to live – or half-live – in an unreal world of fantasy. Again, it is important to deal with these feelings. The most tragic thing that can happen is that to save the parents from the full force of their disappointment, they have another baby straight away and bring it up to be a 'poor substitute' for the one who died. I have met and worked with many such victims of old tragedies in my time as a psychotherapist, and they each deserved better from the people who claimed to have loved them and to have wanted them to come into the world.

16
Loss of a Parent

It can be harder to grieve for a parent than for anybody else. The reason for this is that so few of us ever get to know our parents as real people with whom we can be on equal terms. Some of us, for example, never feel at ease addressing parents by their first names; some of us wouldn't even dream of doing so. Yet the use of such names is a normal prerequisite of all other apparently close relationships. Our parents are the people we have known longest, and this would, in any other relationship, increase our chances of knowing them best. But where parents are concerned, how long we have known them has nothing to do with how well we know them. Perhaps because they belong to a different generation, perhaps because their own parents did not encourage familiarity, perhaps because they hang on to the power that parenthood brings, or maybe because we are reluctant to stop seeing them as anything but parents, there seems to be a barrier between us and them which prevents equality and real friendship.

It is much easier to start our grieving when the person we have lost was somebody we felt close to and could accept and love as an equal. It is hardest when we have felt afraid of that person, or angry with him or her, particularly if we have frequently been forced, by the power that person wielded, to do what he or she wanted even though this was not what we wanted, or needed to do. Many parental relationships are like this. Yet people think of them as normal and acceptable because they have never known any other kind. And there is a whole apparatus of myth and propaganda to prevent further questioning of the power of parents. We are taught that love is natural between child and parent, so we feel that there is something unnatural about us if we do not love ours. We are threatened with some of the severest punishments of childhood if we should ever be disloyal to our parents. It is our duty to love them. There is nobody else in the whole world but parents and children who would even remotely imagine that they could love one another out of duty. Of course there are exceptions – men, women, and children who get to know one another and to love one another equally and without obliga-

134

tion, even though they are also related as parent and child. Maybe these are not the exceptions, but the generality. If so, then most grief for a parent is no harder to begin than any other grief, and no more difficult to complete. That would be difficult enough.

Yet where there is a special difficulty, and when an adult knows in his or her heart that less than a full grief was experienced at the loss of a parent, this can be extremely difficult to talk about openly. People are shocked at the thought of a son or daughter hating a parent, particularly if that parent has just died. They can find it extremely offensive for somebody to say that he or she was in some way glad the parent died. Even to express indifference – 'I don't care whether he dies or not' – sounds cruel and callous, particularly when somebody says this about his or her own father. There is a taboo placed on honesty about parenting which keeps many people from saying openly what they feel, and this stops them facing the full reality of what they have lost when a parent dies.

Perhaps because I meet through my work only those people who admit to having difficulty, perhaps because the work I do enables people to say things to me they would not say openly in a more public setting, the impression I have is that the overwhelming majority of people never grieve fully for the loss of the real people their parents were. The loss of a parent seems to me to be one of the most significant experiences of anybody's life, yet it is also probably one of the most dishonestly described. So if you, in your own grieving for a parent have felt that you could not talk about what you felt, and could not even compare it with the real feelings of other people to see whether you were 'normal' in your reactions, then I can assure you that you are not alone in this. Knowing about some of the feelings that I have had described to me may help to give you a starting-point for a realistic reappraisal of what you have lost when your own mother or father died.

Only when I deserved it

Mike – not, of course, his real name – is typical of one group of people who feel unable to grieve for the parent they have lost. I met him several years ago as part of a consultancy project for the company where he worked as a senior manager. He was powerfully built, a very positive man, one of the people who seem to combine the ability to drive other people with the kind of inspirational leadership which makes them enjoy the experience. He is now a very successful managing director. We were talking quite casually after a hard day's work, when he said he did not want to consult me as a psychologist, but something was puzzling him. His father had died four years ago to the day, and he wondered why he had never wept. It wasn't because he felt that big boys don't cry, or anything like that, he said. He had 'wept buckets' when his mother died. He believed it was good for people to cry and to grieve for those they loved. But he had never 'been able' to cry for his father.

What emerged as we talked further is that he had very much enjoyed his relationship with his father. He described him as a person he 'respected', rather than loved. His father had taught him a great deal about life, taking him on camping and rock-climbing trips, often tackling cliff faces with him that stretched Mike's ability to the limit. Mike was often very scared, but he knew he had to keep a cool head and get out of scrapes by himself. Once, he said, he had slipped and nearly fallen to his death. 'It was a miracle I got out of it', he told me. 'The Old Man just sat there and watched. Even when I reached safety he said nothing – just nodded and lit his pipe. I loved him for it. No fuss, no bother. No praise, either.'

I asked Mike if his father had ever punished him, and I shall never forget his reply. 'He broke one of my ribs once,' he said, 'when I was ten. I'd given him some lip or something, or cheeked my mother, so I must have deserved it.' I asked how he felt about this now, but there was no sign of anger or fear or disapproval from Mike. He respected the Old Man. For my part I felt I knew why Mike had never wept for him.

Mike is typical of quite a large group of people who are brought up to be tough, unsentimental realists. This is achieved by one parent – usually the father – teaching them through fear and anger to take their punishment and bounce back regardless of how they feel. If they complain they are told that 'life's like that – you'll come up against far worse when you're older.' They are taught respect, and if they are lucky, they are given respect too. But respect is a long way away from love. You only get respect if you deserve it, and if you fail there is nobody to pick you up and kiss you better. I think Mike, and many of the less lucky people who are trained this way – including those who failed to bounce back – have difficulty grieving for their dominant parent because they did not love the person who bullied them as children. If they met their parent as equals at all, it was only to take a slight rest before the parent found another challenge where he would be superior and the child was forced to strive to catch up.

So why did Mike describe his relationship as one of love? One reason is that he had very little choice but to accept what his father did and to evaluate it positively. Anything less than wholehearted support for his father, anything less than enthusiastic acceptance of each little bit of punishing challenge, would have been evidence of abject failure, and his father made plain many times that he had no use for 'failures'. He would have been totally ignored by his father – or constantly sniped at and ridiculed by him. Another reason is that Mike had no way of knowing that there was any other kind of father. What he felt must be love! And throughout all this, mother never intervened. Perhaps she was scared too, or perhaps she felt it would be best for Mike if she said nothing. Either way, his love for her was genuine enough for him to weep when she died.

Relief not sorrow

Elaine's mother seems to have dedicated her life to making Elaine unhappy. She had been dead just over a year when I met Elaine, a member of a training group I was working with. 'When she died, and ever since she died, I have felt nothing but relief,' said Elaine. 'I am glad she's dead. In fact, when I knew she was really dead, I could hardly believe it. I danced for joy – literally got up and danced and sang. Her death is the best thing that has ever happened to me.'

For some people there is a significant element of relief when a parent dies – and not just when the death releases somebody who is much loved from a long and painful illness. The relief comes from the knowledge that a lifetime of being 'put down', systematically degraded, and constantly being humiliated is over. This is what had happened to Elaine. The details are unimportant – indeed, they would be misleading, since without Elaine telling the story, they would sound like a collection of trivial incidents. There had been no physical violence, only a constant and unremitting violation of Elaine's right to feel good about anything she did for herself. It was all done, moreover, in the name of motherly love. Elaine was told each time mother 'helped', that 'my daughter is useless and always has been', or some equivalent version of the same message. The saga was a very long one indeed. I felt after more than three hours of listening to it that I still had heard only a fraction. Yet there was very little dramatisation. It was a catalogue of facts in my opinion, not a vengeful narrative from an unstable person. Elaine was telling the truth.

It was mainly because she had been so unhappy as finally to seek help that Elaine had begun to understand that her mother really hated her. This had happened just before her mother died, and in one sense Elaine's reaction to news of the death had been so dramatic because it had coincided with the final stages of her realisations about what had been done to her by her mother. It was how she would have felt at any time on hearing that her mother had died. But she might otherwise have been more restrained about how she expressed her feelings. I have met many people who felt some of what she felt. But Elaine is the only person I have known who felt free enough to celebrate her relief.

The white lie

Sometimes the son or daughter is controlled by the parent by means of the 'rescue' system. For example, they are told not to do this or that because it 'might upset your father' or it 'gives me a headache'. If they do what they want to do, even into adult life when they are quite capable of judging the consequences of their own risks, they are told that this has hurt or upset one or other parent, and the implication is that they must not make the same mistake again.

The man I shall call 'Paul' is one of the multitude of people who are brought up this way. He felt permanently responsible for his mother and father's happiness. At times this diminished, and at other times grew stronger. Not that he realised this until he came to talk about feeling guilty when his mother died and he had not wept. The immediate cause of his guilty feelings was probably something many other 'rescuers'

138

have experienced and not understood.

What had happened was that the last time he had seen his mother was when she was due to go into hospital and was almost certain to die there. His father, typically, had made a great fuss, but no practical arrangements. It had all been left to Paul. But the most important part of what was happening was that Paul's mother was not to be allowed to know how seriously ill she was. Paul went along with this. When his mother said goodbye, as she was taken to the ambulance, he tried to reassure her. 'I'll see you soon,' he said. 'You'll be back home in no time at all.'

It was no more than the kind of white lie that was always used in his family to control things which were embarrassing or painful or just a nuisance. And at the time he said it, although he knew it was not true, he felt that it was necessary and right to rescue her from the distressing facts. It was only later, as he explored a vague and yet powerful feeling of guilt that he recalled the remark. Then he said that he had not been able to weep for her since she died. I asked him how he felt about lying to his mother. 'I was just doing my job,' he replied. Then he cried. 'I didn't want her to die. But I couldn't tell her that.'

There was a great deal for Paul to work through from that moment. The reality of what he had lost when his mother died was – like many of our closest relationships – a mixed reality. Over the next few months, however, he found that he had untied a small log-jam of guilt that had been holding back a great pool of anger at the way he had been treated by his parents. He was able, a little at a time, steadily to see through this anger to the truth that lay under it, and then to drain most of the destructive emotion away. He rediscovered his mother as a person in her own right, and eventually began to accept her, not as a responsibility or as somebody he wanted to change, but as a loving woman he knew and liked.

As I worked with Paul in session after session during that time, something else became apparent. From the start of his teen years, Paul had begun to resent the way his parents used him to rescue them from unpleasant feelings. He felt angry that they could not accept him as a person in his own right, when things could have been so very different. But what he hadn't realised was that he had become so frustrated by this that he had given up. He had accepted as a reality that he would never really know his parents. To try to get to know them was a waste of time – a part of his life that was not worth living. In other words, he had begun to grieve for his loss of a true and honest relationship with them.

I think a lot of people do this. They try to get to know their parents, and to get them to accept an equal relationship. But their parents refuse to stop being parents, so some of the love which they had for one another dies. Mike's love for his father, and Elaine's for her mother – the love which they had felt as babies – was killed off by their own parents. So was Paul's love for his mother and father. This is a severe loss – and like all significant loss, when it happens to us, we grieve. When Elaine's mother died, Elaine had long ago stopped grieving for her mother, and had begun to hate her. When Mike's father died, Mike had also started long before to grieve for the loss of what might have been a very loving friendship with his father – but, unlike Elaine, he had not gone far enough to see that he really disliked the man. And Paul had also begun to dislike his parents – but still felt responsible for them. So Paul had been grieving for what-might-have-been, for the honest friendship he had wanted and could not get. He had started this grief as a teenager, years before his mother actually died. And he had to finish this grief first, before he could start the grief at what he had actually lost by his mother's death. Only when what-might-have-been was completely dead, and its death accepted, could he tackle his grief for what-really-was.

Never very close

'I never felt close to either of my parents', is a sentence I have heard many times when asking people about their experience of grief. The man I shall call Nigel, a research chemist, in his early forties when I met him, seems representative of many of the people who say this.

Nigel's father was a university lecturer, and his mother had grown up in a country vicarage, the only child of an elderly cleric and his shy young wife. Both Nigel's parents were kindly and caring. They took a keen interest in his welfare and wanted him to succeed and to be happy. He was fond of them, but tended to take them for granted. They encouraged him with his schoolwork, and were pleased when he won a scholarship to Oxford. He obtained an excellent degree, then his doctorate, spent a year at an American university, and was eagerly recruited by one of the biggest companies in the UK as a research chemist. When he was thirty, he fell in love with Jane, a librarian almost ten years older than he, and took her home to announce the engagement. His parents liked her, and Nigel and Jane married. His career prospered, and he was put in charge of a team of scientists.

When I met him it was mainly because his company's personnel director wanted to promote Nigel, and the two of them were concerned as to whether Nigel could take on even more man-management. They felt help was needed because Nigel felt remote from the people he supervised. As Nigel's counsellor, I soon discovered that his father had died only a few months ago, and wondered what bearing this had on his need for help, so I asked how he felt. 'I was sad, of course,' he said. 'I shall miss him. But it was no trouble. I never felt really close to him.'

I encouraged Nigel to talk about his father, and that was when the facts outlined above emerged. 'Did your wife like your father?' I asked at one point. 'Yes,' he said, 'only she commented that he and my mother and me never touched. I hadn't noticed till then, but it's true. I can't remember being touched by either my mother or my father. I suppose they must have done so when I was a baby. But not after that.' 'Did you cry when he died?' I asked. 'Not really,' said Nigel. 'It didn't seem right somehow. As if it would have embarrassed him.' 'Him?' I asked. 'It would have embarrassed me. But Jane cried,' he answered.

Parents who hardly ever touch their children, and take a kindly but remote interest in them are not uncommon. They are 'loving' parents in their own way – certainly not brutal and violent. But they are oppressive in their own way, too. They are often people who feel very uncomfortable about free, exuberant, and spontaneous sexuality. They oppress – or 'suppress', which means the same – their own animal needs, and thus prevent their children from learning how to express the natural warmth and loving spontaneity which goes with a child's need to be loved. Their children play very seriously, have fun earnestly, avoid rough-and-tumble contact, and dislike any form of casual touching, however well-meant or friendly. Not surprisingly, they grow into people who cannot use a major part of their equipment for expressing feelings – their skin.

I asked Nigel how he had felt when Jane cried. 'A bit put off,' he replied. 'I never can see why people make such a fuss at funerals.' I'm not sure if he ever will. Maybe Nigel will never know what he has lost, and, as the old saying puts it, 'you can't miss what you've never known'.

Rite of passage

The death of a parent is an important event for each of us in that it means we have lost somebody we might have loved, and who had probably the greatest influence on who we are and what we do with our lives. Maybe, like Mike, Elaine, and Paul – though probably unlike Nigel – you 'lost' the person you might have loved, the real person your parent was as a fellow human being – a long time before your parent actually died. Or maybe – like Peter, whose mother said goodbye before she died, or as in Josie's dying – a new relationship between parent and child became possible for you before bereavement.

The element of personal loss when a parent dies, however, is not the only item which causes difficulty for those who mourn. From time immemorial, part of the Indo-European culture tradition has been that the death of the dominant parent signals a transfer of power and authority to some successor. For example, when a father dies, it can mean that the eldest son then takes over as head of the family. Property may have to be redistributed amongst the children. There may be a dependent surviving parent – a subordinate mother, for example – who now becomes the responsibility of the children. What is to be done about this person? Who looks after him or her? It is important to note that this too is a question of the disposal of property, particularly where the surviving parent was almost totally dependent economically, socially, emotionally, and physically on the parent who died.

So, part of your own grief at the loss of one of your parents might have been suppressed due to the behaviour of the rest of the family, and due to squabbles over who takes over or who inherits property. After a parental death, families reorganise their power structure. You can opt out of this, or join in. You may also have a new chance to get to know your family better, so that part of the power system can be dismantled and replaced by real love. For example, some people find that parental death helps them heal long-standing disagreements with brothers and sisters, or provides a new basis for developing a real understanding on equal terms of the surviving parent. The loss of a parent is also an important part of your own growth. Out of the complete grief-work that you do, you can achieve a new sense of your own maturity. You may feel more alone than ever before. You will have to stand alone now, and take more responsibility for your own life. It is this feeling of aloneness that many people take into crisis when their parents die. By accepting it they say goodbye to part of the dependence of childhood, and become more adult in their own right.

So far we have looked at the loss of a parent in terms of the adult child and the more elderly parent. Sometimes, of course, the parent dies when his or her child is still very young. Maybe your own mother or father died during your childhood. Or maybe you need to help children through their grief at the loss of a parent. What are the special problems caused by parental loss in childhood and what can we do for them?

It is important first of all to underline several of the things that have been said earlier on. First, children are people. They are not especially more resilient, as is sometimes claimed, or less resilient than any other group of people. Nor are they, just by virtue of being children, any less intelligent or more intelligent. They are individuals, and each has his or her own individual capacity for understanding what has happened in his or her own terms. They feel things the way adults feel them, but the power structure that surrounds any individual can prevent expression of feelings, and this applies equally to children. Secondly, children have the same need as adults to complete their grief-work. The reality of what a child has lost needs to be accepted, they need help – and they are also faced with the task of deciding whether to reduce their commitment to life, or to extend it. A grieving child also needs to resist isolation and to decrease its dependence on the person who has died.

The best way to assist a child to grieve has already been described in the last chapter. In principle, there is no difference between grieving for your own life or for the loss of somebody who was a major part of that life. The worst way is to drive grief underground by not allowing the child to talk about his or her feelings, or insisting that they be talked about your way, rather than his or hers. If you are grieving yourself at the same time, then you need extra help with your own grief so that you will have time to enable your children to share their grief with you, and not have to shut them up because of your feelings. Avoid 'double-grieving' – trying to do the child's grief-work for him or her. And do not rush the child. It takes every bit as long for a child to complete grief as it does for an adult. Just as it may take you all your life to understand and accept, so with him or her.

If your own parent died when you were a child, and you can remember the mother or father you lost, then circumstances could have led to a lot of your grief being held back. You may now be able to weep for him or her. You may also be able to say goodbye – perhaps for the first time. Remember that people we say goodbye to are special people, people who can come and go as they please, who are always welcome to return. So if you miss your mother or father, even if it was years ago that he or she died, tell him or her out loud, and say goodbye, and acknowledge any anger he or she caused you, and any fear you felt because he or she left you when you needed a parent to look after you. If you can let your parent go, and live in peace with him or her, then all the energy you have saved up over the years against their return can be spent on the living – yourself and those who need you.

17
Living with Grief

Grief plays a much larger part in our lives than most of us realise. This is because we tend to think of grief only in connection with bereavement. Grief, in fact, is the way we respond to any significant loss, and there are many other kinds of significant loss we may have to come to terms with through grieving. For example, there are many people to whom the loss of employment is a severe setback, threatening not only their economic security, but also their sense of their own value. It isn't just people who have been dismissed, or made redundant who can be affected this way. It applies equally to many who retire from work, whether they do so earlier than they ever expected, or at the scheduled age. The breakdown of a marriage – whether or not it leads to separation or divorce – is also a major loss for many of those who experience it, including their children. Indeed, severe disruption of any important relationship, such at that between brother and sister, or parent and child, can cause lasting damage to those affected, and lead to permanent and bitter estrangement. When this happens people grieve for what they have lost.

The need to adapt to the fact that life will never be the same again also affects that very large group of people who, as a result of global conflict in recent decades, have been driven from their homelands. In our time there are millions of people who have lost the freedom to live where they were born, to speak the language they first learned, and to follow naturally the customs of their forefathers. And there are many amongst them who will grieve for this loss for the rest of their lives.

Physical loss affects many people, too. Accident or surgery can drastically alter the range of things a person is able to do. The amputation of a limb, the loss of sight or hearing, extensive disfigurement, the removal of a breast – all these events can mean that life will never be the same again in important ways. If such things happen to us, we need to adapt the best way possible, to come to terms with the changes forced upon us, and to grieve for what we have lost.

Of course, life isn't just a catalogue of tragedy. We don't spend all our time being knocked flat by economic, social, or physical disasters. Most of us have our fair share of hard knocks, and go through periods when we feel miserable or helpless, frustrated or anxious, but we bounce back one way or another. We can look back on happy memories, or feel good about present fulfilments. We can gain deep satisfaction from the steady construction of future attainments. We have people, and places we love, activities that absorb us and reward the effort we put into them.

When life is generally good, we tend to think of the problems we meet as minor interruptions in our happiness, to be ignored if possible, and to be dealt with if there is no other choice. We think of major tragedy as something other people experience. It won't happen to us. And if it does, we'll face it when it happens. There's no point in worrying till then, we tell ourselves. In this way we neglect our ability to respond to loss until we need that ability – not realising how much we need it to be kept in working order. When the hard knocks arrive, they hurt us far more than they need to. And that ability to do better than cope with life's problems is our capacity to grieve well – to tackle the tasks of grieving without delay, distortion, or unnecessary prolongation. If we fail to understand how to grieve, if we neglect our ability to carry out the tasks of grief when we are faced with relatively simple problems, then, when the big tragedies strike, we are likely to be hurt more than we need, to hurt others whom we need not hurt, to stay hurt for longer than we need.

Living with grief, then, means rather more than simply recovering from bereavement – although this is never simple, and never easy. It also means having a day-to-day capacity for adapting to both great and small losses using only the energy appropriate to that loss, not getting things out of proportion, not being permanently damaged by anything that can happen to you or the people close to you. Maybe you have this ability already. Maybe you haven't. Either way, it can do nothing but good to understand what it really means to live with grief, and to get better at it, not just as a preparation for the unseen tragedy that might be lurking around the next corner, but also as a way of being more alive and more yourself as each day brings its ration of rewards and disincentives. How can we use our understanding of grief to achieve this?

Life tasks

As we saw right at the beginning of our journey together, grief serves all the purposes of our lives. In one sense this means that a person who is grieving is presented with the tasks of his or her life as they have always been, but made more difficult because of bereavement. But we can also look at this another way. Even when we are not reacting to a bereavement, we have certain life-tasks to carry out. These tasks are of fundamental importance if we are to do more than merely stay alive and be blown this way and that way by all the changing winds of fortune. If we carry them out on a day-to-day basis we can really be alive in every sense of this word.

The tasks I refer to are the acceptance and resistance tasks we have already considered many times. To be really alive, for example, we need to be able at any moment of our lives to accept the full reality of our being. This is by no means easy for us to do, and we need to be aware of the difficulties and how to tackle them. We also need to test our commitment to life, and to do so as a normal part of being alive. Every day brings large or small opportunities for us either to reduce, to maintain, or to enhance our commitment. It isn't easy to recognise all these opportunities for what they are, or to live in such a way that we go on steadily increasing our commitment to life. We are likely instead to spend at least a part of our lives doing things we feel we have to do but don't want to do, and feeling that a part of the life we have is not worth living.

The third major life-task we are faced with concerns help. When should we seek it? On what terms should we offer it? These are not trivial questions, but issues of principle that lie deep within our value systems. Do we, for example, help other people regardless of the cost to ourselves and our families? What is our responsibility towards the community we live in? Can we trust everybody when we need help? In accepting on a day-to-day basis the need we have both to give and to receive help, we are bound to come up against major questions of morality and ethics. We also test our inner sense of worth, our value to ourselves as well as our value to others.

Resistance tasks are no less important. So far we have discussed resistance in terms of two separate tasks – the need to resist isolation, and the need to resist dependence. But both are really two different ways of looking at the same need, the need to 'be' with integrity. Integrity is the completeness of the person within his or her limits. If we become too dependent upon another person or on a set of circumstances then we lose part of our integrity. We become a mere colony of that person instead of a country in our own right. We submit to that person's judgements, carrying out his policy, not our own. We shelter under his or her defences, and neglect to build our own. We stop being complete, and this loss of integrity is never fully compensated for by the little bit of safety and the little bit of purpose we gain.

At the same time, to become too isolated also means we lose integrity. When we withdraw from other people, when we cut ourselves off from them and say we do not need them, we are deluding ourselves into thinking that there is such a thing as a complete person who doesn't need anybody. If we do not need other people we are not complete. We are probably scared or angry or both – but even a recluse needs people to be scared of, angry with, or to worry about. Isolation is the cause and the effect of a damaged capacity for love. We isolate ourselves when we feel unloved or incapable of love. And isolation makes matters worse. It forces us to damage still further our ability to be lovable, and makes us even more incomplete than we were before.

In our daily lives, then, if we are at least to maintain, and at best to enhance our commitment to life, we need to find some kind of balance between dependence and isolation. We need to be independent enough, and un-isolated – involved – enough, to keep our integrity. If we get this wrong then we will be lonely, unloved, unloving. Or we will be eating somebody else's resources at their cost, or being eaten by somebody else at our own expense. Somewhere between the two extremes of parasite and hermit we can be ourselves, asking and giving help, knowing why we live, and realistically appraising the rewards and the disincentives of being nobody else but ourselves.

We are used to the idea that these tasks are difficult when our need to face them comes from bereavement. We are not so used to seeing them as part of our response to other forms of loss, nor as part of our response to life itself. But that is what they are, life-tasks we are not used to thinking about. So we fail to recognise just how important they are, and how difficult it is to work at them. Because of this we often do them badly, and fail to realise the potential of our own lives. A few examples of the way people respond to loss other than bereavement will help to illustrate this point.

Loss of structure

Over the last decade, for all sorts of economic and political reasons, the pattern of work in western societies has altered quite dramatically. This has led to a situation where loss of a job has almost become a commonplace. For a great many people – particularly for men who grew up with expectations of a career, and who have the responsibility of financial support for a wife and children – the loss of employment is a severe blow. Everybody to whom it happens is faced with a set of tasks, the life-tasks we have been considering.

None of these tasks is easy, and they do not present themselves in a neatly arranged order of priority. One of them is the need to accept the reality of what has happened. If all you had to do was nod when you received your dismissal notice, and then walk straight into another job, it would be simple. But for most people it is not like this. The news comes either as a surprise or as a relief, but always as a shock. Very few people avoid a phase of doubt and questioning. Is it really happening? Why me? Do I deserve it? What will happen to me and my family now? Will I be able to get another job at the same money? Fear, anger, and worry usually follow, as with any other grief reaction. The fear is often connected with a sense of failure, a feeling that the loss of a job is just punishment for lack of ability. For some people it is a fear that at their age they will no longer be attractive to other employers. Often there is also a fear that other people will not understand.

Anger is also a normal part of the response. It may be anger against the government, the company, or against a particular manager who seems to have been ultimately responsible. It may be anger that is turned inwards and becomes self-punishment, to be experienced as feelings of guilt. In many cases people feel a need to cry, partly in fear, partly in anger. And there are many who find themselves unable to put all their energy into finding another job because so much of it is being spent on swinging between fear and anger. They are too worried to become effective decision-makers. In the early stages this may even stop them telling wives, husband, or parents what has happened.

Job loss is also usually accompanied by a feeling of loss of belonging. Work provides an important addition to our identity, and to our security, but it also gives us a place where we belong. When you lose your employment, you lose this too. Accepting this part of the reality can be very difficult. Particularly if it has been part of your daily pattern of behaviour for many years to go to work, to do your job, and to come home at more or less the same time every working day. You do not belong at home at such times. You feel like an intruder, and this reawakens feelings of fear and anger, and loss of identity. Work structures our lives, and the loss of that structure, taken for granted in the good times, is hard to realise. It is added to by a loss of specialness – for so many of the skills you have no longer mark you out as differently valuable from everyone else. People who are used to working and find themselves unemployed or retired often feel that they are now just part of a vast faceless crowd, all equally helpless and lost, none of them special, each of them 'just another unemployed person'. Yet each has to combat this feeling sufficiently to keep his or her skills alive, and to look different enough to be able to compete successfully with other candidates for a new job.

The need to resist isolation is also just as important in reaction to loss of employment as in bereavement – and it may be just as hard to meet. We can become isolated by feeling that nobody else understands, and that the people who used to understand us, our former colleagues, are gone for ever from our lives. Our relationships change too, as they do after a bereavement. People we used to think of as special no longer seem as close or as concerned. We 'realise' who our friends are. And we need to resist the isolation of living in somebody else's territory, so that they think of us as a nuisance, and add to our sense of rejection when they make this clear. This often happens to husbands who retire or become redundant, and 'get under their wives' feet'. But resisting isolation can be carried too far, so that the alternate danger increases, and we become too dependent upon others. We can find ourselves

150

getting more attention by failing to find a job than by succeeding. We can become used to having more time to enjoy ourselves.

If work meant you used to neglect your children, and you can now spend more time with them, it can be hard to want to return to a way of life where you see less of them. In the search for a new job we can become too dependent upon re-emphasising our old skills, too reliant on the view of what we are good at that others have given us over the years, so that we do not strike out imaginatively on our own, or try for jobs we could do, but which would mean a change of career pattern.

Partly because very few of us think of job loss as to do with grief, and partly because few of us understand grief in any case, the reaction to loss of a job is not as widely understood as it might be. So the kind of help people really need is often unavailable. Instead of being enabled to reassess life-tasks, instead of having access to non-directive counselling, unemployed people find themselves either ignored or hectored. This is no different from telling somebody after a bereavement to pull themselves together and stop feeling sorry for themselves. It might work in a minority of cases. But for most people it makes the task of recovery without loss of commitment to life far harder. The bitterness, the resentment it builds up, will take a long time to dissipate. Growth is set back, not encouraged. The waste it causes is unnecessary, too.

Cause to grieve

The extent to which loss of a job is followed by distorted, delayed, or prolonged inability to adapt obviously varies very widely. As with grief after bereavement, the person suffering the loss may have an extra level of difficulty to cope with. Sudden job loss, like sudden bereavement, requires a different speed of response, and may be more of a shock. Unemployment which was foreseen long in advance, and where there is time for the person to realise the extent of the loss before it takes its full effect, also has different elements of difficulty. And there are bound to be other problems than simple job loss when a person resigns out of anger or fear.

All this applies to other circumstances where we may have

151

to face grief-work without bereavement. If your marriage breaks up, you will need to spend a long part of your life realising what you have gained and lost – not just from the actual divorce or separation, but from the marriage itself. You will need to reassess your need for help, and to find a way forward which increases what you get out of life, rather than diminishes it – and to do so without getting yourself 'rescued' and ending up just as dependent as before, or finding yourself isolated and unloved for the rest of your life. Sudden, unexpected loss of a marriage, and slow, long-anticipated loss again bring an added level of difficulty, as does the break-up which is precipitated by acute anger or fear. We could apply the same analysis to any form of loss. Whatever our cause to grieve, the same life-tasks are thrown into prominence and made more difficult. And they are made even worse when we have neglected them for a long time. If we live in a fantasy world, unaware of the reality of our own value, only fractionally committed to life, unable to seek help, isolated or dependent, then we cannot grow in wisdom, and we shall never collect nor redistribute to others the rewards of a complete life.

Index

JOHN RYLANDS
UNIVERSITY
LIBRARY

154

16 JUN 1986

Living
With Grief

You may have recently lost someone you loved. Or
you may be the relative or friend of someone who is
bereaved, and want to help. Perhaps you are having
to face up to your own approaching death.

Grief is always difficult, and often plunges people
into a deep despair. Dr Lake's very sympathetic
book describes all the different aspects of grief
following bereavement. He shows how it progresses
through 'phases' and how people can work their way
through grief and come to terms with it. Eventually,
the result of a properly completed grieving is a deeper
awareness of the value of life.

Dr Lake also includes special chapters on sudden
loss, suicide, the death of a child, and of a parent,
and offers help for those who know they are dying.

£3.95 net UK only

ISBN 0 85969 426 7

A Sheldon Press Book

Sheldon Press, Marylebone Road, London NW1 4DU